BOOMER
VOLUNTEER
ENGAGEMENT
Collaborate Today,
Thrive Tomorrow

Jill Friedman Fixler and Sandie Eichberg,
with Gail Lorenz, CVA

Foreword by Marc Freedman

In partnership with VolunteerMatch

Edited by Beth Steinhorn

D1379545

AuthorHouse™
1663 Liberty Drive, Suite 200
Bloomington, Indiana 47403
www.authorhouse.com
Phone: 1-800-839-8640

In partnership with VolunteerMatch
www.volunteermatch.org

Book design by Lisa McGuire
Communication & Design
Phone: 719-486-1584

First published by AuthorHouse 5/1/2008

Library of Congress Control Number: 2008903957

ISBN 9781434385901

Printed in the United States of America
Bloomington, Indiana

This book is printed on acid-free paper

To Baby Boomers, who are the future of nonprofits, and to the nonprofit leaders who will engage Baby Boomers to achieve each nonprofit's mission, vision, and dreams.

CONTENTS

FOREWORD

After retiring from a 20-year career as a credit union manager, Jeanne House began to explore her options. She became a docent at the Star Spangled Banner Museum, then began working on a research project with the United Methodist Women to understand why children fail in school.

"One day a letter came to my home, announcing the need for tutors in local schools," Jeanne explains. "I thought, 'Why is this coming to me?' And then I knew—the right place for me was in the classroom, helping children to succeed."

Jeanne joined Experience Corps, a national program that engages people over 55 in solving society's greatest challenges, beginning with literacy. Jeanne joined to try her hand at helping struggling students learn to read, but, like many other Experience Corps members, she got hooked. She's been working in Baltimore schools with 300 other Experience Corps members for four years now, accepting more responsibility—for the success of the students and the program—each year.

"I listen to the children, really listen. I know that if you let a child feel that someone really cares, they will learn," Jeanne says. "And I know that if I am helping one child, it makes all the difference."

Jeanne's story says so much about Baby Boomers and twenty-first-century volunteering. She was searching for greater fulfillment and purpose in her life. She wanted to continue to grow and learn. She wanted to make a real, measurable difference. And she wanted to use her talents to solve big problems, to leave a mark on her world and on the next generation.

Nonprofit leaders, concerned by a slide in the number of dedicated volunteers, can learn so much from Jeanne—and from this terrific book.

Boomer Volunteer Engagement: Collaborate Today, Thrive Tomorrow makes a vital connection between the desire of Boomers for social purpose and the need of nonprofits to survive and thrive. This guidebook provides a map for nonprofits that want to move beyond the limits of staff-driven organizations. It explains exactly how to transform volunteer roles to engage Boomers and how to keep them interested.

Those who adopt the principles in this book will help create a new model for the second half of life, but more important, they will reap the benefits of Boomer energy, experience, and talent to meet their missions. They will reach more children, build more affordable homes, treat more sick people, and engage more allies to support their work. They will be better positioned to succeed.

I salute the authors of this book. With nearly 10,000 Boomers turning 60 every day, *Boomer Volunteer Engagement* comes not a moment too soon. There's a new workforce for social change out there, just waiting to be engaged.

Jeanne House knew when she was in the right place. If you're reading this book now, you've found the right place, too.

—Marc Freedman
Founder and CEO of Civic Ventures,
and Co-founder of The Purpose Prize and
Experience Corps

ACKNOWLEDGMENTS

Legions of Baby Boomers have inspired us to see that their cohort can be the abundance of resources that nonprofits need to thrive and grow. We are grateful to them, and to others who believe in our vision. This book would not be possible without the support of Rose Community Foundation in Denver, Colorado, who awarded us an innovation grant to complete the book as part of their Boomers Leading Change initiative. We are thankful to our colleague Sarah Christian, Director of Strategic Partnerships at VolunteerMatch, who championed the book to her organization. We have been inspired by our partnership with the VolunteerMatch organization. Their support, wisdom, vision, and kindness to us have been expressed in countless ways. VolunteerMatch's commitment to quality volunteer experiences is nothing less than inspirational. Our thanks also go to Atlantic Philanthropies for their generous support of VolunteerMatch and Rose Community Foundation's Boomers Leading Change initiative.

Our deep appreciation goes to Marc Freedman for writing the foreword to this guidebook. His work in both *Prime Time: How Baby Boomers Will Revolutionize Retirement and Transform America* and *Encore: Finding Work That Matters in the Second Half of Life* was the inspiration for this book. We believe, as Marc does, that the social legacy of the Boomer generation is an invaluable and abundant resource for all.

We would be remiss if we didn't thank other colleagues who have helped us along the way. Scott Martin has been a cheerleader and has generously shared his cutting-edge ideas on Boomer volunteer engagement. Marilyn MacKenzie has graciously allowed us to use her Motivational Analysis from

The Volunteer Development Toolbox: Tools and Techniques to Enhance Volunteer and Staff Effectiveness. Marlene Wilson, an early leader in the profession of volunteer administration and the unofficial godmother of volunteer management, set in motion the journey that has led us to create a model for volunteer engagement.

This book began with conversations with friends and family. It grew to reality thanks to the brilliant editing of Beth Steinhorn, who found structure for our work, brought refinement and clarity to our words, and shared her passion for volunteer engagement. Our talented designer Lisa McGuire created a sophisticated and easy-to-navigate guidebook. Our colleague Jennifer Rackow not only added a fresh perspective, but generously shared her expertise in performance measurement and her article from *Volunteer Management Review,* "The Individual Volunteer Plan: Developing Top Volunteer Talent." Her conviction that volunteer engagement is the key to nonprofit capacity building has fueled intense discussions and new insights into this model. Linda Puckett, our organizational goddess, has supported and assisted us throughout the monumental process of completing this book.

A special thanks to our husbands, children, and friends, who supported us and gave us wings to pursue our dreams.

Introduction

Imagine a world in which your nonprofit organization has all the resources it needs to serve more clients, deliver more programs, strengthen its staff, spread its message more widely, and increase its financial stability. Envision a future in which nonprofits have a pool of talented, skilled, and passionate individuals on call to build organizational capacity by serving as consultants, strategists, marketing gurus, ambassadors, innovators, mentors, fund-raisers, and direct service teammates. If this vision attracts, excites—even inspires—you, read on, because this future is here, now. This abundant resource is a workforce 78.2 million strong; they are the Baby Boomers, the former flower children born between 1946 and 1964,[1] and they are our strongest growing resource.

Boomers have led change in every phase of their lives—from the revolutionary social changes during their teens and young adulthood in the 1960s and 1970s to the unprecedented career mobility and the ongoing presence of women in the workforce that marked their professional lives in the 1980s and 1990s. Just as concern for society's well-being was the root of the social movement of the 1960s and 1970s, a desire to take care of individuals, the community, and the earth will propel Boomers to revolutionize nonprofits in the twenty-first-century. Boomers desire and know how to positively impact a nonprofit's capacity more significantly than any cohort of volunteers that has preceded them. They are redefining retirement and will demand changes in the very nature of volunteerism.

To prosper and to leverage this resource, nonprofits must reengineer volunteering to align Boomers' skills with organizational vision, mission, and goals in a purposeful way. Gone forever are the gray-haired men and women who, after spending forty years at the same job, became reliable volunteer office assistants and crossing guards. Boomers want to be challenged. They want to leave a social legacy. They understand the need for traditional volunteer positions that fulfill basic needs, such as filing, answering phones, and staffing an information desk, but they desire more. They want a variety of community service options so they can choose the ones that best fit their interests and their busy lives. They want to know that they have an impact on the organization's vision and mission. Nonprofits can capture the talents and skills of Boomers and the next generations when they transform volunteer management into volunteer engagement and thus grow their capacity beyond the limits of what staff alone can accomplish.

While nonprofits are beginning to feel the effects of this dramatic change in the demographics of their volunteer pools, most organizations are not yet equipped to adjust to the impending transition—let alone seize the opportunities that the shift offers. Nonprofits have undergone many changes over the past several decades. Many have successfully implemented concrete performance measurements and adopted more sophisticated fund-raising and marketing strategies. However, the traditional model of volunteer recruitment, retention, and recognition has not changed significantly. Nor has the culture of limited resources and staff. We refer to this mindset as the "never enough" syndrome. How many times have we heard staff and leaders lament, "If only we had more staff!" Or, "We could reach more clients, if only we had more resources!" The very challenge posed by potential Boomer volunteers is, in fact, the answer to the common perception of "never enough."

With a cohort of potential volunteers 78.2 million strong, finding a way to engage these highly skilled, passionate individuals with profound circles of influence in a meaningful way is the key for nonprofits to transform the culture of "never enough" to one of "abundant resources."

A New Vision for the Future

The authors of this book are Boomers with a combined seventy years of experience working as volunteer management professionals within the nonprofit sector. We have been volunteer managers and consultants in cultural, government, health, animal welfare, and religious organizations, and hospitals. We have founded and managed small and large volunteer programs and have trained hundreds of new professionals in the field. As practitioners, we have helped the field evolve toward an organized approach to engaging volunteers. We have watched and participated as new technologies continuously open new worlds and change the face of volunteerism and the definition of community. Online social networking is already key to engaging the Boomer volunteer and is only going to become more integral as more and more Boomers participate in these online communities of people with shared interests and activities.

We have learned over the last ten years that what worked before does not work now; the old model of volunteer management does not jibe with what Boomers want as volunteers.

In the process of writing, we realized that the volunteer engagement concepts advanced in this guide reach beyond Boomers; they apply to all the generations that follow. We must turn the concept of volunteer management on its head in order to engage today's volunteers and the abundance of resources they possess. The very theory of volunteerism must be transformed from managing volunteers to engaging them powerfully in communities of action to result in remarkable impact and change.

Times have changed since 1976, when Marlene Wilson published *The Effective Management of Volunteer Programs*[2] and created the modern volunteer management movement. That book suggested that "management skills of the highest order" were an effective method to plan, organize, staff, direct, and control the volunteer workforce. Greatest Generation (Americans born between 1911 and 1924)[3] and Silent Generation (Americans born between 1925 and 1945)[4] volunteers flourished in this system. It matched their need to give their time with the needs of nonprofits for labor. Baby Boomers' central motivation is different: they want to impact mission and vision, and they want to accomplish it on their own terms.

The journey that we outline in this guidebook will take organizations to a new place. Through deep collaborations with Boomer volunteers, nonprofits will position themselves to meet the demands of the twenty-first-century work environment. Throughout the guidebook, we explore new language to advance volunteerism to a position that melds with present-day organizational realities. Current volunteer management language reflects a top-down philosophy: recruitment, interview, placement, retention, recognition, and performance evaluation; all these

The first Baby Boomers turning 60 are the same generation that John F. Kennedy famously challenged to ask themselves what they could do for their country. This same generation is now positioned to lead another social movement based on sharing life experience. They couldn't come at a better time.

—Civic Ventures/Met Life Foundation, New Faces of Work Survey 2005

terms imply that staff is directing the action to or on behalf of the volunteer. The volunteer is the object of the action.

We embrace a new vocabulary to reflect more accurately the philosophy and practice of collaborative volunteer engagement:

From		To
volunteer management	➤	volunteer engagement
recruitment	➤	cultivation and networking
placement	➤	negotiation and agreement
supervision	➤	support
performance review	➤	performance measurement
recognition	➤	acknowledgment
retention	➤	sustainability

The shift in language reflects the grander shift in attitude, philosophy, intention, and action. Reengineering a nonprofit to engage Boomers successfully as volunteers is a demonstration project for a broader discussion of what volunteer engagement means for nonprofits today and in the future.

The Process for Redefining Volunteerism

Transforming volunteer management into volunteer engagement requires the commitment, dedication, and patience of organizational leaders and volunteers. The process takes time and hard work—but the benefits are immeasurable.

This guidebook opens with "Understanding the World of Boomers," an in-depth look at the unique nature of the Boomer generation. The next chapter, "Structuring for Innovation," outlines the foundation for organizational transformation and the process for convening a task force to shepherd the change. The chapters that follow provide a step-by-step process for reengineering an organization's relationship with volunteers and include tools and exercises that will concretely move the organization forward in volunteer engagement. Each chapter features the philosophical framework for the step, the implementation process, and exercises for staff and volunteers to complete and add to the organizational toolkit.

The Implementation Steps:

- **Mapping the Initiative:** Work Plan
- **Creating the Opportunity:** Position Descriptions
- **Developing Connections:** Networking & Cultivation
- **Capitalizing on Boomer Resources:** Motivational Analysis
- **Creating the Collaboration:** Interviewing & Finding the Fit
- **Nurturing the Relationship:** Support
- **Sustaining the Collaboration:** Ongoing Engagement

These steps are guided by the same principle: nonprofits have access to all the resources they will ever need because of their profound circles of influence. The key is transforming the organization to a culture of meaningful volunteer engagement in order to access those abundant resources. We recognize that institutional transformation as significant as we are proposing takes an investment of resources and experimentation. Read through the text now. Share the book with your organization. Together, refer to the guidebook and use the exercises to accomplish the paradigm shift we advocate.

By following this process, nonprofits will prosper in the demands of the twenty-first-century environment. In this new future, nonprofit leaders and staff will work collaboratively with volunteers to achieve organizational goals and build organizational capacity in ways they cannot now even imagine. Boomer volunteers (and, likely, all volunteers) will be viewed as a resource for skills, talent, passion, and renewed energy for the nonprofit sector.

We invite you to join us on a journey to harness Baby Boomer volunteer power. Be bold and audacious as you experiment with the tools and strategies we offer. You can be sure that the reward of working with Boomers is a worthy venture with incalculable benefits.

The United States today possesses the fastest-growing, best-educated, and most vigorous population of older adults in the history of the world. The whole structure of volunteerism is about to be reinvented. There exists a virtual tidal wave of skilled professionals, talented individuals, and top drawer executives who are ready to do good.

—Edgar Bronfman,
The Third Act: Reinventing Yourself After Retirement

HOW TO USE THIS BOOK

This guidebook presents a step-by-step process for creating a culture in which Boomer volunteers will thrive in your organization. Its structure is designed for easily finding your way through the book and through the process of reengineering your own organizational structure and practice.

In Chapter 2, you will establish your team and assess your current volunteer engagement practices. In the following chapter, you will develop a Work Plan for this process. The companion Progress Report at the end of each chapter guides you through the learning from that chapter and enables you to track your advancement.

Chapters 2–9 have a common structure with sections identified by icons.

KEY CONCEPTS 🔍	Each chapter begins with key concepts.
[THE FRAMEWORK]	We define the contextual background in this section.
✓ MAKING IT HAPPEN	Steps and exercises are provided in this section.
PROGRESS REPORT	Chapters end with a Progress Report.

The final chapter, "Sustaining the Collaboration," includes a review of all the concepts and provides the opportunity to track progress and begin planning for the next steps to mission and vision fulfillment.

We have included a glossary to define new terminology and a resource list for further learning. The exercises that appear throughout the guidebook are marked with an icon ⚙⚙ and blank templates of each exercise are included in the appendix for you to photocopy and use as you and your organization create a fully integrated culture of Boomer volunteer engagement. Additionally, the exercises and templates are available as downloadable PDFs at www.BoomerVolunteerEngagement.org. Some are interactive PDF forms with clickable fields and can be saved on your hard drive.

CHAPTER 1

Understanding the World of Boomers

Baby Boomers have grown up, but they have not lost the idealism of their youth—
though it is often buried under layers of responsibility to family and career. Research by
Civic Ventures, VolunteerMatch, Rose Community Foundation, the Corporation for
National & Community Service, The Points of Light Foundation, and others cries out to
leaders of nonprofits to rethink the ways volunteers support their organizations.[5] Before
launching a comprehensive plan to reengineer organizational volunteer engagement, it
is crucial to understand Boomers and what makes them tick.

Leaders of volunteers who adhere to the traditional volunteer management model
may think that Boomers are uninterested in volunteering because they reject traditional
volunteer roles. In truth, most Boomers drop out of their volunteer assignments only
when their expectations for volunteer service do not correlate with the reality of the
current volunteer workplace. Boomers who are leaders of industry are rarely interested
in low-impact volunteer positions. Boomers who grew up with flextime in the workplace
expect and prefer flexible volunteer schedules that few nonprofits offer. Boomers whose
careers were marked by unprecedented mobility expect a veritable buffet of volunteer
options. Almost every survey of Boomers and nonprofits reveals that large numbers of
nonprofit leaders believe their organizations are ready to engage Boomers, and equally
large numbers of Boomers say that nonprofits are operating in ways that discourage
them from volunteering.

Boomers have a multitude of choices of how to spend what their parents called the leisure years. Volunteering is but one option. According to the think tank Civic Ventures, Boomers will redefine the second half of life as a source of social and individual renewal. They see it as a new adventure—a time to travel, take classes, and, if the nonprofit sector is lucky, to serve a higher purpose and create what Civic Ventures calls a social legacy.[6]

Researchers and authors have written a great deal about Boomers utilizing volunteering as an anchor for the next part of their lives. In his book *Encore: Finding Work That Matters in the Second Half of Life*, Marc Freedman champions late-life careers in the nonprofit sector.[7] *In Leap! What Will We Do with the Rest of Our Lives?* Sara Davidson documents her struggle to find purpose as she moves through her 60s.[8]

Nearly 30% of Boomers will seek avocational and vocational opportunities within the nonprofit sector in either encore careers or volunteer settings, according to 2007 studies by Colorado's Rose Community Foundation[9] and VolunteerMatch (a study focused exclusively on its million-plus users).[10] Boomers in their late 40s and 50s are volunteering at higher rates than members of the Greatest Generation and Silent Generation did at the same age, according to the Corporation for National & Community Service's report *Keeping Baby Boomers Volunteering*. Boomers were volunteering at lower rates than their predecessors while in their 30s, but that trend reversed as Boomers reached their 40s and 50s. The report attributes this increased volunteerism to high education levels and a later average childbearing age. Research shows that adults with school-age children living at home are more likely to volunteer than those without school-age children at home.[11]

The 78.2 million Baby Boomers are a virtual gold mine for nonprofit organizations. The first Boomers turned 60 on January 1, 2006.[12] Between 2011 and 2029, Boomers will reach the traditional retirement age of 65 at the rate of about one every eight seconds.[13] The number of volunteers 65 and older is projected to increase 50% by 2020 and to balloon 100% by 2036, according to the Corporation for National & Community Service, which calls their estimates conservative. This means volunteers in their mid-60s and older will grow to 13 million in 2020 from today's nearly 9 million. When the youngest Boomers turn 65 in 2029, the ranks of 65-and-older volunteers will swell to 18 million.[14]

A social revolution—possibly as important as the one led by Boomers in the 1960s—will occur if nonprofits strategically engage Boomers in high-impact collaborations that build a nonprofit's capacity to fulfill its vision and mission. Just as they did over forty years ago, Boomers will lead the way to a new era.

Who Are Boomers?

Boomers are indeed a unique group. They have challenged and redefined social structures throughout their lives, and they are doing it again in how they address retirement. They are expected to live longer and retain their health longer than any previous generation. They will not be put in the rocking chair; they will remain in the driver's seat. They will decide how, when, and where they will retire, reside, spend their money, and spend their valuable time.

Boomers are the most educated and financially secure generation in history. They will be the recipients of the largest transfer of wealth in American history when their parents die. This amount is estimated at a staggering $41 trillion, about $6 trillion of which will go to charity, according to a 2003 study from the Boston College Social Welfare Research Institute.[15] Historical data indicate that a volunteer's connection to the nonprofit leads to more dollars donated. According to the Independent Sector's paper "Giving and Volunteering in the United States" (2001), volunteers give twice as much to nonprofits as nonvolunteers.[16]

Boomers are not simply extending their years working and volunteering; they are doing work that adds deeper meaning to those years. In *Encore: Finding Work That Matters in the Second Half of Life*, Freedman writes that Boomers are not like the previous generation that looked forward to freedom from work when they retired. Boomers dream of "freedom to work—in new ways, on new terms, to new and even more important ends." A plethora of options and responsibilities compete with volunteering for their time. They may want to travel, continue their education, cycle in and out of the workforce, or launch new careers. Caregiving for parents and grandchildren may be a priority. Financial needs to continue paid employment with long hours tether some Boomers to the workforce. However, nonprofits can reignite the Boomers' 1960s idealism and channel it to promote social welfare.[17]

Boomers are sophisticated consumers who are accustomed to choosing among an abundance of options and consider time a limited commodity.

—Dwight Denison and Ashley Moore, "Using Baby Boomers to Expand Nonprofit Capacity," *Journal for Nonprofit Management,* 2007

Knowing Boomer demographics—particularly how they see careers and what inspires them—will help nonprofits develop inviting organizational structures.

- Boomers are expected to live longer and retain their health longer than any previous generation. They are also the "Sandwich Generation," simultaneously caring for children and aging parents.[18]
- Boomers are more educated, healthier, and wealthier than any preceding generation.[19]
- They are far more computer savvy than previous generations.[20]
- They have vast social networks.[21]
- Four out of five Boomers report that they expect to work past the traditional retirement age of 65 years.[22]
- Younger Boomers (born 1957–1964) continually change jobs.[23]
- They work long hours.[24]
- Retirement is not an event. It is a metamorphosis that may take ten to fifteen years.[25]
- They have more freedom in selecting encore careers.[26]
- They may take a year off after retirement before they are ready to volunteer.[27]
- Boomers are motivated strongly by impact. They want to see results.[28]
- Their top volunteer motivator is passion for a cause. Many researchers predict Boomers will reengage in social activism because Boomers want to feel productive.[29]
- They expect to leave a social legacy.[30]
- Boomers want lifelong learning opportunities.[31]
- They are not joiners of social organizations, preferring to create their own connections.[32]
- They are avid consumers who expect choice and flexibility.[33]
- Boomers are eager to utilize their workplace skills when they volunteer; this is especially true of Boomer men.[34]
- They believe their workplace skills are what nonprofits need most.[35]
- They want encore careers in the nonprofit sector.[36]

By welcoming Boomers and younger generations as collaborative partners, nonprofits can:

- Ensure a future volunteer corps for the organization.
- Expand the organization's pool of skills, expertise, and other human resources.
- Widen the organization's circles of influence.
- Strengthen the ability of nonprofit professionals to ultimately fulfill the organization's mission.

The focus of volunteerism moves beyond the chores of today to the efforts that are necessary for the organization to survive and thrive in the future because of what Boomers can accomplish.

Boomer volunteer engagement builds capacity beyond the limitations of what staff alone can accomplish. Imagine what could happen if volunteers were asked, "What is the skill that you possess or wish to learn and would be willing to share with us to accomplish our mission?" and if the nonprofit was poised then to engage those individuals in ways that utilized those skills and interests. For example, instead of entering numbers into a database for the accounting department, a volunteer who is a CPA led a task force to examine and update accounting procedures.

Boomers' skills and experiences increase organizational impact and outcome beyond what staff alone can accomplish. Boomers have access to a wide range of skills, experiences, and perspectives to draw on in fulfilling vision and mission. When they involve entrepreneurial Boomer volunteers, nonprofits benefit from the intellect of those who can take an idea from conception to implementation and high-quality, cutting-edge service delivery. For example, volunteers who previously had been asked only to work at fund-raising events for a violence prevention agency were invited to use their professional skills as social workers, lawyers, and psychologists to collaborate on a guide to help laypeople recognize signs of abuse. As a result, the guide became a model for other agencies.

Boomers extend the nonprofit's circle of influence. Every nonprofit has a wide circle of influence that includes its donors, board members, staff, clients and their families, neighbors, stakeholders, partners, and existing volunteers. Imagine the possibilities if every person within the nonprofit was asked to network to increase capacity to obtain specific, strategic goals. At an inner-city school, a volunteer classroom aide mobilized her book club to give holiday gifts to the children. At a library,

The Boomers have an average life expectancy of 83 years and have a 33.2% volunteer rate, which is four points above the national average of 29%.

—Bureau of Labor Statistics, 2006

a board member who is experimenting with volunteering before he commits to a master's program in library science organized a task force to catalogue a recent acquisition of books. At a soup kitchen, a retired bistro manager coordinated in-kind donations from restaurants.

Boomer volunteer engagement frees employees to steward critical initiatives and do different work. When volunteers are engaged in impactful work that was once the exclusive domain of employees, those employees are free to pursue their dreams for the nonprofit's success. A social worker at an assisted living facility had long wanted to establish a formal peer mentoring program where long-term residents helped newcomers acclimate to congregant living. When a Boomer volunteered to take over organizing weekly outings, the social worker had time to implement her plan. As a result, the resident mentors gained meaningful work, companionship, and satisfaction as they provided invaluable assistance to new residents. They reported feeling energized and excited by their new roles.

It takes more than a few new strategies and examples to engage Boomers as volunteers. It takes reimagining the role of volunteers in an organization and the possible results of involving volunteers in every aspect of operations. It takes a new philosophy and organizational buy-in from top to bottom and from bottom to top. The next chapter sets the stage for making this profound transition and provides concrete strategies for achieving that buy-in across all segments of the organization.

NOTES & IDEAS

Many Baby Boomers are now experiencing a time of "mid-life crisis." For many, especially men, it is the movement of a mindset from success to significance.

—Elisabeth Hoodless, Executive Director of Community Service Volunteers (CSV), the UK's largest volunteering and training charity

CHAPTER 2

Structuring
for Innovation
Process & Assessment

KEY CONCEPTS 🔍

1. Organizational change happens in three stages: letting go of old ways of doing business, a transitional phase, and an integration of new practices.

2. To be successful, board and executive leadership must fully embrace the initiative for change, model the collaborative approach of Boomer volunteer engagement, and hold staff accountable for this new way of partnering with Boomer volunteers.

3. A Boomer Volunteer Engagement Task Force must include key agents of change (people who connect, share information, and spread the word), visionaries, and individuals with particular skills and expertise.

4. An important part of the first stage of organizational transformation is to assess current practices of Boomer volunteer engagement and identify areas of need and opportunity.

Shifting from volunteer management to a culture of volunteer engagement is a significant move for any nonprofit, one that impacts every facet of doing business and one that will require considerable transition. In his book *Managing Transitions: Making the Most of Change*, William Bridges writes, "It isn't the changes that do you in, it's the transitions." As any organization prepares to make a major transformation such as this, it is essential to recognize the stages of change. As Bridges outlines, organizational change occurs in three stages: the letting go stage, the neutral stage, and the new beginning.[37]

In this view, the process actually starts with an ending. During this opening stage of letting go, it is important to understand where you are as an organization, to recognize and honor that place, and even to allow the organization to grieve the loss of the status quo. Despite being named the neutral stage by Bridges, the second phase is the most nerve-racking for many. Some people may experience grief and loss while letting go of the "old ways of doing things," and most will experience some discomfort during this in-between stage. It is both a time of innovation, creativity, and great excitement and a time when some people experience a lack of definition, chaos, fluid boundaries, and shifting sands. Finally, change ends with a new beginning and new way of doing business. Innovations become standardized, experiments are refined into practice, and plans turn into reality.

Reengineering volunteer management into volunteer engagement takes resources, time, and—most importantly—commitment. A nonprofit with a deep commitment to volunteer engagement, but with limited resources and time, can pilot small steps, slowly building capacity for future steps along the way. Yet a nonprofit with vast financial resources, but lacking commitment and readiness, will only end up paying lip service to volunteer engagement, not achieving true transformation. This, ultimately, will frustrate staff, potential volunteers, and existing volunteers.

For a nonprofit to move from a volunteer management model to one that engages Boomers for the skills and passions they have to offer, the leadership of the organization must fully embrace the change. Board leaders vet the process and participate in aligning the work of Boomer volunteer engagement to the strategic priorities of the organization. The board provides the necessary resources and oversees performance measurement throughout the duration of the initiative and beyond.

The Role of the Nonprofit Executive

When embarking on this journey of creating a culture in which Boomers will be meaningfully engaged, nonprofits must understand where they are currently and be prepared to let it go. A strong leadership team can ease that process by creatively guiding the nonprofit organization to identify where it wants to be by looking at best practices of volunteer engagement and gaining inspiration from examples of Boomers who are currently involved in high-level volunteer work. The act of looking forward engages all stakeholders in the process and buoys staff and volunteers as they say farewell to the past.

Another first step in ensuring successful change is to engage the Executive Director or CEO and ensure that this individual fully understands the possibilities, supports the change, and embraces the process for transformation. For example, when contemplating moving her large national organization through a major shift from traditional volunteer management to cutting-edge, capacity-building volunteer engagement, the CEO of one of our clients had a personal "aha" moment and exclaimed, "So what you're saying is that I am actually the Chief Volunteer Engagement Officer." Of course, we answered, "Yes." While successful organizational transformation does not have to begin at the top, this type of organizational change cannot happen without the senior leadership embracing and championing it, modeling the crucial values of collaboration and innovation, and holding staff accountable for it. In other words, the CEO has to live the role of Chief Volunteer Engagement Officer.

The collaborative relationship between staff and volunteers is critical in creating a culture of volunteer engagement with Boomers and your nonprofit. When the CEO is the Chief Volunteer Engagement Officer, his or her job is to create a staff environment in which the volunteer culture will thrive. It is not enough to tell staff that collaboration is important. It must be demonstrated by the CEO and in every human resources practice. For employees to progress from staff-driven management of volunteers to a collaborative culture with access to abundant resources, the nonprofit will need to establish core competencies for volunteer engagement for staff, such as the following:

The engagement paradigm provides a framework for developing not only the support but also the enthusiastic engagement of the entire organization.

—Richard Axelrod, *Terms of Engagement: Changing the Way We Change Organizations*

Strengthening the Nonprofit

- Responsibility for capacity building shared by staff, board, and volunteers. Capacity building is defined as mission-aligned, focused actions that improve the organization's effectiveness.
- Performance measurement and human resources tied to volunteer engagement.
- Volunteer engagement included in the position description of every staff member at every level, defining each employee's role in building the culture.
- Volunteer engagement included in annual goal-setting with employees, and progress evaluated in the performance appraisal system. When employees are evaluated and rewarded through promotions and merit raises, they will make a serious and deliberate commitment to their role in the culture change.

Optimizing Business Operations

- Communications designed to promote the culture of volunteer engagement to all internal and external stakeholders.
- Information and data collection managed for tracking and evaluating the results of collaborative partnerships and initiatives.
- Quality improvements in meeting management so that face time, or virtual meeting time, is productive and rewarding for all participants.
- All volunteer-related risk management issues addressed as problems to be solved and not as barriers to engagement.
- Technology acumen increased in all aspects of creating the culture of volunteer engagement, including online social networking, research, assessment and tracking, and managing information.

Connecting People

- Hiring practices adjusted to target a candidate's ability to collaborate with volunteers.
- Collaboration and team building supported in the work of the nonprofit.
- Community-at-large engaged to broaden impact.

The Role of the Network

People make change happen. Some people play a bigger role as agents of change than others. While it is critical to have the leadership of the nonprofit embrace and champion volunteer engagement, there are other key people in your nonprofit who will be instrumental in fostering the transformation and inspiring others to get on board. Malcolm Gladwell, in his book *The Tipping Point: How Little Things Can Make a Big Difference,* identifies key players in creating any tipping point for change: Connectors, Mavens, and Salespeople.[38] Connectors are individuals who know lots of people and, most importantly, know how to bring the right people together. As Gladwell put it, Connectors, the people specialists, are "people with a special gift for bringing the world together." Also critical to the process of change are information specialists and "information brokers sharing and trading what they know," the Mavens. Mavens collect information and, more importantly, want to share it. Finally, Salespeople are the charismatic persuaders who are instrumental in convincing others to make change. Cyberspace and social networking sites provide ever-expanding workspace for Connectors, Mavens, and Salespeople.

Each type of influencer is important in creating the culture of volunteer engagement. In Chapter 5, for example, we explore how cultivating volunteers is all about Connectors. For now, consider the role each of these individuals plays in successful organizational change. You want to strategically involve those who bring the right people onto the team (Connectors); those who have inside information on the market, the resources, and the field and are willing to share it (Mavens); and those who will sell the idea and persuade others to join in the process (Salespeople). Who among your staff, board, volunteers, clients, and donors are your most powerful Connectors, Mavens, and Salespeople?

What we're beginning to see is that Boomers are really focused on making an impact through their volunteer opportunities as opposed to volunteering for its own sake. They want to focus on big problems and effective solutions. It's not entirely the way the volunteer community is set up right now. It requires some adjustment.

—John Gomperts, President, Civic Ventures, and CEO, Experience Corps

Organizational change requires the involvement of as many key stakeholders as possible. We recommend establishing a Boomer Volunteer Engagement Task Force to create the vision, shepherd the process, and develop and monitor outcomes. Such a task force should include the CEO and selected board members, staff members, and current leadership volunteers. Because the initiative is about building capacity through engaging Boomers in high-level volunteer engagement, the most compelling way to ensure that staff, board, and volunteers buy in to the initiative is to demonstrate the benefits by modeling staff and volunteer collaboration from the start. When you include Boomer volunteers as members of this Task Force, you intentionally demonstrate the power and potential of Boomer volunteer engagement.

In addition to ensuring strong representation from the board, staff leadership, and volunteers, an effective Task Force will include the following types of people:

1. People who "get it." Individuals (staff, board, or volunteers) who appreciate the power and potential of volunteer engagement, whose faces light up when contemplating the possibilities that Boomer volunteers offer, and who are naturally creative visionaries.
2. Connectors, Mavens, and Salespeople. You want a mix of these different personalities and strengths to round out your Task Force. Each type of individual will have an integral role in the success of the initiative.
3. People who bring important skills to the table, including, but not limited to:
    *   Oversight
    *   Research and assessment
    *   Volunteer cultivation
    *   Volunteer support
    *   Technology and data tracking
    *   Project management
    *   Marketing and public relations
    *   Evaluation
    *   Other skills relevant to your nonprofit

Use the following exercise to consider your existing circles of influence—including volunteers—in order to generate a list of powerful individuals who are candidates for the Boomer Volunteer Engagement Task Force. An effective Task Force will include individuals from most of these diverse categories of skills and strengths.

Boomer Volunteer Engagement Task Force
Brainstorm Exercise

1. Make a list of people already in your circle of influence from your board, current volunteers, donors, clients and their families, partners, and vendors to invite into the planning and implementation process.

2. Of those individuals, whom would you describe as "visionary"? (Who has indicated an appreciation and understanding of the potential of Boomer volunteer engagement?)

3. Of those individuals, who are the strongest Connectors? (Who knows a lot of people? Is skilled at bringing people together? Has an extensive list of contacts and uses it?)

4. Of the individuals, who are the clear Mavens? (Which individuals have information about a topic of importance to this Task Force? Who collects information and likes to share it?)

5. Who from your list are the Salespeople? (Who is charismatic? Who is a persuader?)

6. What are the specific skills necessary for an effective Task Force for your organization? Who possesses this expertise and these talents?

2

Next, prioritize your list and invite those individuals to connect you, advise you, and inspire others about this initiative. Ask them to partner with staff, board, and other volunteers to reengineer the organization's relationship with volunteers. Your invitation to each individual should be carefully crafted and delivered by someone with influence and a personal connection. Carefully consider and prepare what is presented to each individual. Make sure the invitation includes the vision for the initiative and detailed information on why this person is being solicited for participation. An invitation could sound something like this:

> We value your skills and the way that you can envision a bigger future
> for our nonprofit. We invite you to partner with us as we launch an
> initiative to transform the way we work with volunteers in order to
> intentionally and effectively engage Baby Boomers and all the skills they
> have to offer to our organization. It will be some of the most important
> work we can do to position our organization for the future. [Insert some
> details about this future vision and anticipated impact.] We would like
> you to join the Boomer Volunteer Engagement Task Force because we
> can utilize skills in . . . [insert the particular skills you seek from that
> person] and believe that you will be able to lead this initiative to success.
> Would you participate in our first Task Force meeting next month?

Be certain to include information about the anticipated time frame, the schedule of meetings, and meeting locations—as well as any training Task Force members may receive as part of the project (in addition to the training in volunteer engagement provided by this step-by-step process). Chapter 5 includes exercises and tips on developing case statements and messaging designed to cultivate volunteers into positions such as the Boomer Volunteer Engagement Task Force.

Once you have your Task Force team in place, the first agenda item is to engage in some research—often known as "discovery." This process is designed to appraise the nonprofit's current status in terms of volunteer engagement and basic plans, initiatives, and needs. To start, each team member should complete the following Assessment of Organizational Volunteer Engagement tool individually and then compare answers.

The assessment tool will uncover some surprising facts and pinpoint opportunities for change. Nonprofits that imagine they are volunteer friendly may find that they are not. Nonprofits whose volunteer base is shrinking with the exit of Silent Generation and

Greatest Generation volunteers will discover reasons why Boomers are staying away. Staff may think everything is fine; volunteers may disagree. The tool will show that there are new ways of thinking even within the volunteer management model. It will help you look more critically at the process and see what is possible.

Assessment of Organizational Volunteer Engagement

YOU . . .	Score 1 if you . . .	Score 2 if you . . .	Score 3 if you . . .
Organizational Support for Volunteers			
Involve volunteers in all aspects of organizational life.	Have staff and/or a few dedicated volunteers do most of the work.	Have a volunteer presence in all aspects of organizational activities and programming.	Mandate that staff and leadership utilize volunteers in their work.
Allocate resources, including budget, space, and tools, for volunteer engagement.	Assume that volunteers are "free" and do not require resources.	Have a budget for volunteer resources.	Reflect in your annual budget detailed expenses for volunteers, including supplies, space, software, training, recruitment, staff time, and recognition.
Train staff and board leadership to work effectively with volunteers.	Assume staff and key leadership know how to work with volunteers.	Reflect responsibility for volunteer engagement in staff and lay leadership position descriptions.	Provide formal training to staff and lay leadership on how to work with volunteers.
Needs Assessment and Program Planning			
Have defined why volunteers are a strategic priority for the organization.	Use volunteers for activities and programs as they are needed.	Have identified volunteers as leaders and helpers in moving the organization forward.	Have a written philosophy statement about volunteer engagement that identifies volunteers as an indispensable channel for ideas on organizational direction and operations, programs, and activities.
Include volunteer engagement in risk management planning.	Do not consider volunteer assignments in your risk assessment.	Evaluate all volunteer assignments for risk.	Have appropriate insurance for volunteer engagement and evaluate/update as necessary.

YOU . . .	Score 1 if you . . .	Score 2 if you . . .	Score 3 if you . . .
Effective Recruitment and Cultivation			
Have written position descriptions for all volunteer assignments.	Verbally explain to volunteers what they are going to do.	Have a position description for each volunteer assignment.	Conduct an annual (at minimum) review and update of all position descriptions.
Have a process for volunteer cultivation.	Do recruitment exclusively through announcements in the newsletter, website postings, etc.	Figure out who knows prospective volunteers and have them do the recruiting.	Have a written strategic recruitment plan for all volunteer assignments and needs.
Maintain current and accurate records on volunteers.	Do not track volunteer involvement.	Have a record of all volunteers and what they do for the organization.	Integrate volunteer records with membership and donor information.
Interviewing and Placement			
Design volunteer assignments for a wide range of skills, ages, and interests.	Rely on a specific group of volunteers (e.g., stay-at-home mothers, retired, etc.) to get the work done.	Include all age groups and demographics among your volunteers.	Design assignments specifically to reflect a wide range of skills and interests and not limit work to clerical and administrative positions.
Screen and place volunteers in assignments that are right for them and the organization.	Let anyone volunteer for anything.	Match volunteers to the assignment that aligns with their interests.	Recruit volunteers based on their preferences, the skills they willingly share, and the relevant qualifications for the job.
Orientation and Planning			
Have written policies and proce-dures for volunteer engagement.	Assume that volunteers know what is accept-able for them to do.	Have some policies that relate to volunteer involvement.	Have detailed written policies and procedures and orient all volunteers to these guidelines.

YOU . . .	Score 1 if you . . .	Score 2 if you . . .	Score 3 if you . . .
Supervision and Support			
Hold volunteers accountable for what they do.	Cannot fire a volunteer.	Clarify for volunteers the limits and boundaries of their assignments.	Have staff and leadership follow up with volunteers to make sure they accomplish what they set out to do, releasing them as needed.
Actively solicit volunteer input in decisions that affect them.	Have volunteers do whatever they are assigned.	Encourage current volunteers to give feedback.	Have a system in place for collecting and reflecting on volunteer feedback on decisions that affect them.
Strategies for Sustainability (Retention)			
Have volunteer assignments that are meaningful and that impact the ability of the organization to achieve its mission.	Design volunteer assignments around having people do the work of the staff and/ or board of directors.	Design volunteer assignments to have an impact on the mission of the organization.	Reflect a diversity of work in volunteer assignments, from direct service to program delivery, and incorporate high-level assignments, such as the provision of professional services.
Ensure that staff and leadership recognize volunteers informally and formally.	Host an annual recognition event for volunteers.	Give frequent recognition to volunteers from the board, staff, and other volunteer leaders.	Acknowledge the successes of volunteer endeavors in personalized ways through sharing celebratory information in collateral materials (e.g., the website, newsletters, announcements, emails, and written materials), through letters, and through customized networking opportunities with organizational leaders and others.

Key

Do you score mostly 3s? If so, you are well on your way to having an outstanding process for Boomer volunteer engagement. Your organization understands the benefits of a culture that embraces and celebrates volunteerism.

Do you score mostly 2s? Then your volunteer engagement process has room for improvement. Look at the number 3 answers to see where you have opportunities to improve your volunteer engagement practices.

Do you score mostly 1s? It is not unusual to start developing a volunteer engagement strategy from the ground up. Identify specific ways to develop greater competency in volunteer engagement and nurture volunteer talent.

The results of the Assessment of Organizational Volunteer Engagement provide a snapshot of where your nonprofit stands right now in terms of Boomer volunteer engagement. They are your initial benchmarks. The lower-scoring areas point out strong candidates for change. If you scored mostly 3s, congratulations! You already have a strong baseline of volunteer engagement practice. As your Task Force debriefs this exercise, consider these questions:

- What are your strengths?
- What surprised you most about the results?
- What will you have to do differently to raise your scores to all 3s?
- Do you have volunteers aging in place?
- How is your volunteer landscape changing?
- Can you project how your organization will score on this assessment if you change nothing as Boomers and the generations that follow begin to dominate the volunteer workplace?
- Are you positioned to meet Boomers' evolving needs for flexible schedules, high-impact volunteer roles, and collaborative relationships?
- What were your "aha" moments and why?
- What are the biggest challenges for you in making changes for quality improvement?
- What are you willing to invest (time, money, people, etc.) in this process?

Now is the time for additional research to supplement the Assessment of Organizational Volunteer Engagement results. Make certain that all Task Force members understand the current state of the nonprofit. Are they familiar with the strategic plan? Have they read the annual report? Do they understand the climate in the communities your nonprofit serves? Do they know which issues and causes are "hot" and which new initiatives and grant proposals are currently on the table?

You may employ multiple research instruments at this point: focus groups, surveys, interviews, audits, and more. You should tailor your research to the needs of your particular nonprofit. Regardless of the methods, the goal is to establish benchmarks by gathering information on the current state of volunteer engagement and organizational capacity for fulfilling its mission. These benchmarks will be used in the near future to measure progress. The research will also provide context and inspiration for planning your pilot programs by identifying areas of need and opportunity. The research phase may take a few weeks or up to two months. It will be worth the investment of time and energy.

Once you have established your baseline of practice and clarified organizational priorities, the next step is to apply this information in identifying your nonprofit's needs for volunteer assistance. The following Needs Assessment exercise is a useful tool for helping your Task Force members see what is possible when volunteers are engaged in building the nonprofit's capacity to address the dreams and challenges it faces. As a group, review and discuss each question on this Needs Assessment. This is the first step toward letting go of the past and establishing a vision of a more expansive, sustainable future.

1. What are the dreams for your organization that require more people, expertise, money, or tools to accomplish?

2. What are the problems and challenges that your organization is currently experiencing?

3. What is your nonprofit currently doing that you would like to increase, replicate, or expand?

4. What is an area of your division/ department that is always underutilized or understaffed, or seems constantly overloaded?

5. What specific skills and resources would your organization's personnel need to fulfill your dreams? To meet its challenges?

6. Who in your circles of influence embraces volunteers and would be open to building the organization's capacity to address these dreams and challenges?

7. Who are your Mavens? Who are the
   experts on volunteering? Who are the
   experts on projects your organization
   wants to begin or complete?

8. Who are your Connectors? Who seems
   connected to everyone in particular
   communities you want to tap? (Which
   communities?)

9. Who are your Salespeople? Who can
   sell someone the shirt off her back and
   make her glad to buy it?

10. Are you an answer to any of the
previous three questions? (Which
ones? Why?)

11. With what could your organization
utilize a consultant or specialist to
help you—now and in the future—
work toward vision and mission
fulfillment?

12. What areas of your organization
would benefit from program outcome
evaluation?

Based on these Needs Assessment data, what are three entrepreneurial volunteer assignments or volunteer leadership positions that would be an asset to you and your organization?

1. _____

2. _____

3. _____

Armed with this invaluable information about the current state of your nonprofit and its needs, you and your partners for change are ready to embark on a journey to a new future for your organization—a future of limitless possibility. Your team has begun to dream a new vision, and your next step will be to map out your route. In the next chapter, the Task Force will begin the exciting process of developing a plan to make this vision a reality.

CHAPTER 3

Mapping
the Initiative
Work Plan

KEY CONCEPTS 🔍

1. Pilot programs can transform organizations gradually, intentionally, and effectively by creating learning opportunities and leveraging internal champions.

2. A Work Plan establishes the vision for Boomer volunteer engagement, identifies action steps, and provides indicators for performance measurement.

3. Progress Reports are a tool to measure the changes made by the Boomer Volunteer Engagement initiative and a way to communicate the impacts to key stakeholders.

Organizational change can happen in many different ways. Leaders often try to transform their nonprofits rapidly, implementing sweeping, simultaneous change across their organizations. There are mandated initiatives, collaborative models, and change management models. In our work with Boomer volunteer engagement, we have found that the most effective and long-lasting organizational change happens when a nonprofit first embraces a structure in which change can be innovated and managed in increments by a small subset of the organization in an effort to engage Boomer volunteers successfully in new, high-impact capacities. These "pilot" initiatives enable faster rollout and results assessment. They are nimble—responsive to changing circumstances and adjustable at nearly any point. Because of their limited initial scope, pilots are often perceived as lower risk and less threatening, especially in more established, mature organizations. They also enable organizational leadership to choose the individuals and groups with the greatest probability of success, and to collect concentrated data to evaluate the pilot program.

In large organizations, the pilots could involve a few chapters, affiliates, departments, or program groups; in small organizations the pilot may simply be a select program or volunteer work group or cohort (e.g., marketing ambassadors, volunteer educators, and fund-raising volunteers). The pilots are charged with innovating and then testing those innovations in their nonprofit. As the pilot groups learn from their successes and adjust in response to challenges, the nonprofit advances its transformation and embraces a "learning organization" approach to change.[39]

The pilot program approach offers many variations that can be tailored to a particular organization's culture, size, and character, beginning with the pilot selection process. Pilot groups may be invited to participate or encouraged to apply for selection, based on predetermined criteria. Some nonprofits use this as an opportunity to encourage entrepreneurial thinking and planning and even award project grants to selected departments, chapters, or program teams to apply toward their proposed plan. Regardless of the method of selecting pilots, the advantages are the same. A pilot program approach:

• Establishes a learning organization: improvements are made incrementally, with multiple opportunities for feedback and adjustment along the way. Pilots make changes by learning what works for them—and then teach their colleagues in the rest of the organization.

- Leverages your champions: by carefully selecting your pilots, you can begin with your "champions"—the organization's existing innovators, risk takers, and most open-minded practitioners—and, by rewarding them for their ingenuity and creativity, the organization will nurture that spirit of innovation and openness.
- Creates internal publicity: the pilots serve to spread the word about the initiative through the entire organization.
- Uncovers and enhances replicable practices: participants discover best practices that can be replicated throughout the organization.
- Stimulates momentum: with appropriate communication, the successes of the pilots inspire the rest of the organization to innovate as well—and those successes can be highlighted and, in turn, fuel momentum in other areas.

For two examples of discrete pilot projects, see the sample plans on pages 50 and 51.

The gap between vision and current reality is also a source of energy. If there were no gap, there would be no need for any action to move towards the vision. We call this gap creative tension.

—Peter Senge, *The Fifth Discipline: The Art and Practice of the Learning Organization*

Work Plan

A Work Plan is essential to any change initiative. The Work Plan establishes the vision and impact, outlines key action steps, and provides indicators against which leaders can measure progress. Some organizations use a logic model to guide their work; others employ variations of strategic plans or action plans. Our Work Plan is a hybrid of a logic model and an action plan, and incorporates elements key to clear and successful planning. A comprehensive Work Plan includes the elements you see on the facing page.

As a Task Force, develop a Work Plan for your nonprofit's overall Boomer Volunteer Engagement initiative. As you develop your overall Work Plan, the Task Force will define the vision using the action steps in this guidebook. As you flesh out the details of your actions, you will also begin the process of developing the plan for your pilots. What are the discrete projects that will serve as your demonstration projects for the overall Boomer volunteer engagement? To answer this, start by prioritizing your nonprofit's needs as identified through the Needs Assessment. Align those priorities with the strategic plan. Next, determine which of those priorities will be addressed first, through piloting volunteer engagement incrementally. You can use the same Work Plan template as the one developed for the overall organizational change.

On pages 50 and 51 are two sample pilot program Work Plans. One is developed for an internal, operational pilot program focusing on technology upgrades and reengineering. We selected technology because, despite posing challenges to nonprofits, technology is especially important in capturing volunteer information. Also, Boomers expect organized, professional onboarding and cultivation, which can be made more efficient through technology. Many Boomers have technological skills and would be willing to help with such a project. The second sample is programmatic and more externally focused. In this example, an organization is working to develop learning centers at local shelters. The organization has a network of willing community partners but lacks the volunteers to implement this "dream." The Learning Center Team members have high-level professional skills, and the project also has room for people who can pick up donated computers and set them up at a shelter, label books, design the layout of a room, and more. Compare and contrast the entries in these two samples.

As you read these examples, notice the benefits to the organization, the flow from vision to outcome, and the detail of specifics and how they are measured. Using these models, develop a Work Plan for each of your pilot programs.

Work Plan

Vision Statement	Resources	Action	Yield	Initial Impact	Sustained Outcome
Defines the challenge at hand and the purpose and meaning of the entire plan: •What is the need or problem? Or, what is possible? •How do you know? (Research and data?) •How does addressing it align with achieving your strategic goals?	What do you need to have or develop before the action can occur? Be specific and consider: •People, training, and supplies/equipment: Who are the right people? How will you assess their development needs? Who will provide the training? Do you need permission for purchases or contracting? •Money, time, and space. How much? By when? Where will you get it?	What actions need to happen? Add how many, with whom, when, and who convenes and attends, but resist the temptation to describe how the action will happen. •Seminars/events, education, recruitment, fund-raising, outreach, or professional development •Meetings, conferences, and networking internal (policy, awareness) and external •Campaigns and partnership development	Quantifiable results of the action, answering; •How many…? What percentage…? Or, how much…? •What are the baseline numbers resulting from the effort?	Short-term results that demonstrate what is measurably different, often changes in: •Knowledge, skills, or abilities •Behavior or decision making •The most visible manifestations of the problem	Longer-term, lasting results that follow more immediate and tangible changes; these impacts often address deeper roots of the challenge at hand, and: •Changes in condition: economic, physical, social, or political •Create or significantly alter models of doing business •Demonstrate the return on investment in volunteer engagement to all stakeholders

Sample Plan for a Technology Upgrade Pilot Program (Internal)

Vision Statement	Resources	Action	Yield	Initial Impact	Sustained Outcome
Our organization will have a unified, accurate system for all departments to capture, analyze, and use volunteer and donor history, skills, interests, and community connections.	•Boomer Volunteer Engagement Task Force •Time with staff and volunteers who currently use varied record-keeping methods •Work station and Internet access •Basic office supplies •Existing research on volunteer and donor management software and best practices in technology	•Conduct technology Needs Assessment to discover business requirements •Develop Boomer "Tech Team" position descriptions •Interview and place Boomer Tech Team members •Research existing nonprofits •Research tech grants and assistance programs •Write case statement for internal and external stakeholders •Train staff and Boomer volunteers on new system •Evaluate impact	•Number of Boomers engaged (all roles) •One list of business requirements for the technology •One list of potential systems and costs •One presentation to board and staff •Number of staff and Boomer volunteers trained	•Staff time spent on data management decreases by 50% in the first six months •All department outreach lists have an error rate less than 2% by six months after system rollout	•Our volunteer-to-donor and donor-to-volunteer conversion rates both increase by 5% during the new system's first 12 months •System smoothly integrates new events, service areas, volunteers, donors, and modifications to existing records •Data for annual reports, grants, and marketing are available quickly, accurately, and at no additional cost to the organization

Sample Plan for a Learning Center Pilot Program (External)

Vision Statement	Resources	Action	Yield	Initial Impact	Sustained Outcome
We will provide Learning Centers for youth living in our city's shelters. Centers will be equipped with computer stations, books (K–12 level), and furniture—tools to narrow the digital divide and mitigate the risk that these children will spend a lifetime in poverty.	•Boomer Volunteer Engagement Task Force •Shelter partners •Supplies (book labels, computer locks) •Training on shelter youth programming and safety •Existing donor history and interests report for cultivation •Board resolution and strategic plan with Learning Center goals •Shelters' research on current student academic performance	•Develop position descriptions and recruit retired teachers, librarians, etc., for "Learning Center Team" •Write case statement for potential donors •Solicit cash and in-kind donations for books, computers, and furniture (table, chairs, bookshelves) •Collaborate with shelter partners on Learning Center program integration, grand openings, and media where appropriate •Evaluate impact	•Number of learning centers created in 12 months •Number of youth served •Number of Boomers engaged	•Youth attitudes toward reading, school, and computers will improve during the time they are staying in the shelter—as measured by the Garfield Attitudinal Survey •Youth will choose to read during free time at the shelter at least three times per week, as recorded by the Learning Center liaison logbook (current baseline average is 0 times per week)	•Students who live for at least one month in shelters with Learning Centers will be promoted to the next grade on time at a 25% higher rate than the current baseline predicts •Students aged 12–17 who live for at least one month in shelters with Learning Centers will be only half as likely to drop out of school in the next year as the current baseline predicts

Progress Report

As you launch one or several pilot teams, the Progress Report (facing page) is an easy way to share challenges, ask for suggestions, and communicate progress. Over the course of shifting to a culture of volunteer engagement, you will likely report to funders, boards, volunteers, media, and other stakeholders with a vested interest in the success of volunteer engagement pilots. Though they do not have daily operational knowledge of how the shift is going, you can demonstrate organized, specific accountability linked to measurable results, as anticipated by the Work Plan.

Your Task Force now has a record of tools used, pitfalls encountered, partnerships made, and the time it took to accomplish each segment of the plan. Once the team has these results, a very engaging story emerges; that story elevates the conversation from "doing stuff" or "getting through it" to a powerful message about demonstrable results. Participants share a commitment to a specific vision for their engagement, understand why and to whom their engagement matters, and can evaluate whether the purpose of their engagement has been fulfilled.

At this point, you have the support and participation of your organization's leadership—both the CEO and the board. The board provides oversight to the project and engages more Boomer volunteers in leadership capacities. The CEO models high-level collaboration with volunteers, welcomes innovation, and lives the model by serving as the Chief Volunteer Engagement Officer. Your Boomer Volunteer Engagement Task Force is in place, with a collaborative team of key staff and volunteers who are dedicated to dreaming big and innovating new ways of utilizing the resources already in their circles of influence—namely the millions of Boomers who can contribute skills and time to the organization. Plus, you have a Work Plan that maps a route toward achieving a new vision for the future. The following chapters provide more tools and steps, the vehicles that will take you there.

PROGRESS REPORT

Vision: _____

Element	Description	Indicators and Tools	Progress, Challenges, and Needs
Resources			
Action	• Develop a Work Plan for your nonprofit's Boomer Volunteer Engagement initiative. • Identify appropriate pilot programs to advance the initiative and design a Work Plan for each. • Use the Progress Report to begin tracking progress on each Work Plan.		
Yield			
Initial Impact			
Sustained Outcome			

.

CHAPTER 4

Creating the Opportunity
Position Descriptions

KEY CONCEPTS 🔍

1. A well-thought-out, well-written Boomer volunteer position description is the reference point for negotiation, support, accountability, and evaluation.

2. The skills and abilities of Boomer volunteers can increase a nonprofit's scope and reach through high-impact volunteer positions.

3. Innovative volunteer roles and flexible structures for volunteer positions are especially appealing to Boomers and increase Boomer volunteer engagement.

Civic engagement can be the fire in the center of Boomers' lives. It can be a passion when it fits the Boomer's needs on all levels. For Boomers—and the generations that follow—volunteering must thrill them, inspire them, and make them want to come to work as volunteers. It must be stimulating, meaningful, and fun.

Some Boomers want to create their own volunteer positions and some are intrigued by positions designed by the nonprofit. Because no one likes to make a commitment without knowing what he or she is agreeing to do, it is essential that every volunteer has a written position description before beginning an assignment. To avoid misunderstandings later on, the position description should be reviewed by those who will work with the volunteer, as it will serve as the reference point for future negotiation, support, accountability, and evaluation.

A volunteer position description includes the following information:

- Position overview
- Title
- Key responsibilities of the assignment
- Initial impact of the assignment
- Sustained outcomes of the assignment
- Training provided and/or needed
- Support
- Commitment (time and location)
- Desired qualifications
- Desired skills
- Benefits to the volunteer

Position Overview
The position overview is a brief, one- to two-sentence review of the position. It is meant to grab the reader's attention and interest, and is particularly helpful in Internet marketing.

Title
Titles matter. An attractive title is an effective recruitment strategy. Who would want to be a "member of the Marketing Team" when one can be a "Marketing Strategist"? Why

sign up to be an "Office Aide" when another nonprofit is looking for an "Operations Maven"? As long as the position title is accurate (and fits within your human resources policy and standards), be creative about the title and seek input from Boomer volunteers, both existing and potential.

Key Responsibilities

Key responsibilities accurately describe the work of the position, as well as the areas for which the volunteer will ultimately be held accountable. A volunteer who coaches basketball at an inner-city recreation center is responsible for coaching open basketball clinics two afternoons each week at the gym, maintaining the equipment, and creating a safe, mutually supportive environment for teens. A potential volunteer can read these responsibilities and envision himself in this role. It is important that the focus be on key responsibilities and not policy and procedure for the position. If you list more than four key responsibilities, the position may appear overwhelming; only one or two responsibilities may not seem to comprise a substantive assignment.

Initial Impact

Beyond responsibilities, it is important to consider and include the impact of that work. Similar to the initial impact in the Work Plan, initial impacts are the difference these activities will make in the immediate future. For example, the volunteer coach is providing local teens with an activity that promotes physical health and is in a safe and nurturing community.

Sustained Outcomes

Sustained outcomes define the long-term results of the work. Again, like the Work Plan, it is the significant, measurable change in the condition of the organization or the lives of its

Baby Boomers want choice. They want to be presented with a variety of options so that they can pick the one that most closely matches their unique needs. Car manufacturers get this. There are now websites, for example, where potential buyers can create the car of their dreams. You pick the colors; you pick the accessories, all with the simple click of a mouse. Will Boomers want anything less from volunteering?

—D. Scott Martin, "Creating Boomer-Friendly Volunteer Opportunities, Part 1: Restructuring Existing Opportunities," *Volunteer Management Review*

beneficiaries that is likely to continue for the foreseeable future. In the long term, the basketball coach is increasing the teens' likelihood for a physically active lifestyle and has provided mentoring and role modeling that helps teens mature into responsible adults.

When nonprofit leaders consider the potential results of a project, they should ask these questions:

- How can we increase our capacity to fulfill our mission and vision? (With additional volunteer basketball coaches, we can serve more children in need while expanding our programming opportunities.)

- In what ways can our organization increase its scope and range by looking outside of our staff for knowledge, skills, and abilities? (By recruiting a new coach with mentoring skills, the center can expand the impact of the program into life skills development for the teen participants.)

- What are the changes in economic, social, and physical conditions? (As a result of the coaching program, the lives of neighborhood teens will be enriched and they will be better prepared for a productive, healthy future.)

To obtain additional funding, or if the recreation center's potential funders require, a staff member or volunteer leader could potentially measure other specific results of the coaching program, such as:

- Academic achievement
- School attendance
- Attitude (toward reading, school, authority . . .)
- Behavior (truancy, bullying, involvement in extracurricular activities . . .)

Training

Training and development are key in Boomer cultivation, acknowledgment, and support. Virtually all Boomers who have been in the workplace (regardless of what kind of work) have been exposed to professional training. We know from research that Boomers are lifelong learners.[40] By establishing that training and ongoing development are available,

Boomers are more likely to accept an assignment. Training is a persuasive benefit for the volunteers.

Time Commitment and Location Options

It is important to be specific about the time and place demands for the Boomer volunteer. The more flexible you can make the offer, the more likely you are to find the right volunteer to fill the position. This is where the disconnect between what Boomers want and what the organizations offer comes into play.[41] Nonprofit organizations think that an offer of a position is enough to entice the Boomer to their organization. Boomers want to make the choice of when, where, and how they work. The difference is that an assignment with specific routine hours (e.g., Mondays from 12:00 noon to 4:00 p.m.) excludes most Boomers who have traditional employment. On the other hand, when the position is framed as 20 hours over six months, Boomers can see how the position will fit into the demands of their busy lifestyle. One Boomer said to us, "I would much rather be told the time commitment is 52 hours in a year than an hour a week, so that I have control when I volunteer."

If we create the right opportunities, that population [Boomers], which we know is huge, could be enormously significant in helping to solve these problems that are dogging our communities.

—John Gomperts, President, Civic Ventures, and CEO, Experience Corps

Qualifications

As with a well-developed position description for any paid job, carefully strategizing the required (or desired) qualifications is critical. It can make the difference between a long, drawn-out process of weeding through a tall stack of applications from unqualified, inappropriate candidates and a streamlined process of reviewing applications from candidates with the potential to do the work. For seeking a basketball coach to run the biweekly clinics at a downtown recreation center, what types of experience and, most importantly, skills does this coach need? Basketball skills and a certain level of knowledge of the game are important, of course. But what else is critical? Here is where nonprofits need to push beyond the traditional human resources model in which one might simply list "2–4 years, previous experience as a coach" and instead think about skills.

Skills differ from qualifications and basic experience. Skills are proficiencies and talents that may have been developed through unrelated experiences but are transferable. Mentoring skills, teaching skills, ability to work with teenagers, and ability to lead teams could have come from a variety of experiences. The coach would need to be a patient person, and would need a sense of humor. If the position description simply lists "2–4 years, previous experience as a basketball coach," the pool of applicants is significantly narrowed. If, however, the position description focuses on the skills desired, it might attract a retired high school drama coach who was a basketball player in college, or the owner of a local sporting goods store who served in AmeriCorps as a teacher prior to getting an MBA.

Support

We intentionally use the word "support" instead of "supervision." Boomers are not looking for a boss, but a colleague and partner. Defining the level of support for the volunteer from the organization tells the volunteer what to expect. Staff, board members, and other volunteers working with this volunteer also know what to expect, such as "monthly meetings with all peer counselors" or "biweekly check-in meetings with the designated team leader."

Benefits

For many Boomer volunteers, helping the nonprofit fulfill its mission and serve its clients is all the benefit they need, especially when they or someone they know is directly impacted by their volunteer work. We have never met a volunteer who was motivated to volunteer by the annual thank-you event. However, having a "benefit package" demonstrates organizational commitment to the volunteer. Benefits include the things that you do for and with the volunteer, such as thank-you letters to employers, professional development opportunities, and free memberships.

✔ MAKING IT HAPPEN

When generating position descriptions, first take some time to dream. Successfully engaging Boomers just could make those dreams come true. Review the results of your Needs Assessment exercise from Chapter 2, and work as a team to bring some structure to those dreams. How can your nonprofit increase its scope and range through additional knowledge, skills, and abilities? What can be accomplished if resources are unlimited? Developing position descriptions is a way to actualize those dreams.

Consider your current volunteers as well as the vast pool of potential Boomer volunteers. What are their characteristics, and how can their wants and needs fit with the wants and needs of your nonprofit? Gather your team together and complete the following Opportunities for Boomer Volunteer Engagement exercise to explore these big questions.

 ## Opportunities for Boomer Volunteer Engagement

Boomer Characteristic	Strategy	Opportunities in My Organization
Demographics • Late retirement • Long life • Healthy late life • More women wage earners • Sandwich generation • Greater financial resources	• Offer flexible work schedules and locations • Offer short-term volunteer opportunities that have clear beginnings, middles, and ends • Create volunteer positions that can expand as the volunteer has more available time	
Behaviors • Mobile in careers/relationships/locations/roles • Long work hours • Always "on call" for their jobs • Gradual transition to retirement • Less demanding encore careers • Possible sabbatical after retirement and before volunteering	• Create volunteer career ladders • Be prepared for loyalty to a volunteer assignment, not loyalty to the nonprofit • Market your nonprofit to Boomers who may volunteer later	

Boomer Characteristic	Strategy	Opportunities in My Organization
Preferences/Motivations • Passion for causes • Desire to feel productive and see results • Lifelong learners • Want to leave a social legacy • Want autonomy • Want choices • Want collaborative relationships • Want to use their workplace skills • Seek encore careers • Minimal respect for authority • Not joiners of social organizations; create their own connections	• Create an engagement style that is participatory instead of top-down • Encourage Boomers to design or refine their own volunteer positions • Tell Boomers how their volunteer assignments will impact the community • Emphasize impact on clients and other beneficiaries more than impact on the nonprofit organization • Invite Boomers to be involved in organizational change • Offer learning opportunities and provide professional development • Focus on the work, not the process • Empower volunteers to give feedback, take initiative, and recruit others • Celebrate the results of what the volunteer has accomplished • Design rewards that match each volunteer's motivation	

The exercise above is designed to encourage the Task Force to brainstorm strategies to better meet Boomers' desires to cycle in and out of the workforce; have mobility in their careers, relationships, and locations; and pursue collaborative relationships.

The next step is reengineering your volunteer roles and opportunities to think beyond the traditional structures for volunteer positions. Boomers will look for roles that allow them choice and flexibility, but that is not just limited to the number of available positions and the work schedule. Your Task Force should begin to consider "volunteer work" with fresh eyes. Find ways for volunteers to help your organization in new and unique roles that divide and assign work across traditional organizational lines and that fit with the demands of their lifestyles. In traditional volunteer management models, one volunteer fulfills each volunteer position, but there are emerging innovations in the way volunteer positions are structured, layered, connected, scheduled, and shared.

Review the next chart as a group and, in the column to the right, make a list of existing volunteer positions that can be redesigned into new roles and notes on how you would do so.

 # Volunteer Roles

Loosely adapted, with permission, from "Developing Compelling Opportunities for Baby Boomers," training handout, Temple University's Center for Intergenerational Learning, D. Scott Martin, author.[42]

Term Definitions

Episodic	Can be a onetime commitment or occasional participation.
Ongoing Episodic	Volunteers perceive that the assignment is low risk, low commitment, low responsibility, yet they return to the same assignment over and over.
Short-Term	Projects with a beginning, middle, and end, or a project that is very time specific over a short period of time.

Title, Description, and Examples	Commitment	Considerations	Existing Positions We Could Retool and Ideas to Get It Done
Seasonal Work either in the season they are available or the season when they are needed *Examples:* • Snowbirds, seasonal workers • Holiday adopt-a-family, tax preparation	Episodic or short-term Organization's high-season assistance	• Availability • Skill requirements • Connection • Targeted recruitment efforts	

Title, Description, and Examples	Commitment	Considerations	Existing Positions We Could Retool and Ideas to Get It Done
Substitute Provide coverage on an as-needed basis *Examples:* • Emergency child care provider • Legal assistant • Disaster relief	On demand to fill in or be on-call	• Skill level • Availability • Scheduling • Self-direction	
Job Sharing Two or more volunteers share an assignment with either the same responsibilities or complementary responsibilities, depending on their skill set *Examples:* • Any position	Serve as one volunteer sharing responsibilities and splitting the time, providing coverage for each other; schedule can be prearranged or worked out among themselves	• Relationships • Communication • Teamwork • Self-direction • May need to recruit job share partners or have a volunteer recruit own job share partner	
Rotation Volunteers share the assignment by taking turns to accomplish tasks or responsibilities *Examples:* • Snowbirds • Seasonal workers • Part-time employees • Providing coverage for shift work	Specified but negotiable	• Communication • Connection to the organization • Dependability	

Title, Description, and Examples	Commitment	Considerations	Existing Positions We Could Retool and Ideas to Get It Done
Segmentation Divide a new or existing time and/or people-intensive task or position and break it into more manageable specific parts *Examples:* • Special events • Implementation of a program • Rollout of new technology	Negotiated time commitment Can be time limited or ongoing	• Skill level • Relationships • Self-direction • Autonomy • Communication • Ability to work as a team	
Team Volunteering A group of self-directed volunteers taking on a project, program, or assignment *Examples:* • Program evaluation • Research • Shift work • Staffing a client or clients • Families/groups	Time limited or ongoing Episodic or short-term	• Relationship • Community • Self-direction • Accountability	
Consultant Providing professional skills and content expertise to the organization *Examples:* • Strategic planning • Organizational development • Finance • Fund-raising	Usually time limited Schedule based on volunteer availability Could be episodic Could be virtual	• Skill level • Experience • Communication • Relationship • Self-directed • Autonomy • Strategic thinking	

Title, Description, and Examples	Commitment	Considerations	Existing Positions We Could Retool and Ideas to Get It Done
Virtual Providing services to the organization from off-site location, utilizing technology such as phone, fax, Internet, or email *Examples:* • Research project work, such as consultation, mentoring, coaching, technology projects • Training/curriculum development	Schedule own time Time limited or ongoing	• Autonomy • Self-direction • Relationship • Communication • Skill level	

The Task Force is now ready to apply some of the ideas from the Opportunities for Boomer Volunteer Engagement exercise and the Volunteer Roles chart. Prioritize your ideas by aligning the lists with your organization's mission and the needs identified through the Needs Assessment exercise in Chapter 2. Use your new knowledge to draft volunteer position descriptions. Start with writing position descriptions for members of the Boomer Volunteer Engagement Task Force. Following the pilot program model, select a single department or program area in which to write position descriptions and refine the craft of developing them before going organization-wide.

Volunteer Position Description

Position Overview

One or two sentences that give a powerful overview of the position and can be used in recruitment, particularly web-based volunteer matching search engines.

Concepts to Consider

- "Volunteer" denotes who is doing the work; the position title denotes what he/she will be doing.
- A title, in and of itself, can be a motivator or an anti-motivator for volunteer recruitment. For example, "Committee Chair" is not as captivating as "Team Captain"; "Researcher" is not as captivating as "CSI—Community Service Investigator."

Title:

- Distill the responsibilities into three or four key areas that accurately describe what is needed (refer to your strategic plan, if necessary).
- Give prospective volunteers enough information to enable them to envision themselves in the position without feeling overwhelmed.
- Resist the temptation to put policy and procedures into the position description document.
- Limit the key responsibilities to three or four. Fewer than three may feel insubstantial and more than four may feel overwhelming.

Key responsibilities:

- Impact is the difference this activity / volunteer assignment makes. Volunteer assignments must advance the organization's mission, vision, and goals. For example, "The impact of outreach efforts is that 250 previously unknown rural clients will receive referrals to local support services, demonstrating increased access to services."

Initial impact: _____
_____
_____
_____
_____
_____

- Sustained outcome is the lasting impact on the beneficiaries. Using the example above, "The quality of life for 250 clients in rural areas will be improved as indicated by social service agency records of client contacts and actions taken."

Sustained outcomes: _____
_____
_____
_____
_____
_____
_____
_____

- Volunteers want to do a good job and often worry if they will have the skills to perform the job adequately.
- Defining the level of training will help allay fears that volunteers might have about doing the work.
- Training is often a great motivator for volunteers who wish to gain new skills. For example, "All volunteers will receive free training on first aid and CPR" or "on effective public speaking."

Training: _____
_____
_____
_____
_____
_____
_____
_____

- Support defines the supervision that the volunteer will receive. For example, "Each team member will meet every other month for two hours for support from the Team Leader."

Support: _____
_____
_____
_____
_____
_____

- Be as specific as you can in defining the length of time for the assignment: one time, weekly, monthly, total time commitment for the project (months, years), and/ or the amount of time needed for the project (weekly, monthly, annually).
- State when the project can be done: evenings, weekends, weekdays, or "anytime."
- Identify where the work will be done: at home, at the office, off-site, or "volunteer's preferred location."
- The more flexible you can make the assignment, the easier it is to recruit for the position.
- Avoid the temptation to undersell the commitment. It is better to be realistic about the time commitment than to have volunteers become overwhelmed with the work and leave their assignment before it is completed.

Commitment:

Length of time:

Amount of time:

Specify evenings, weekdays, weekends:

Location of volunteer assignment:

- Define what you are looking for in terms of skills, behaviors, and willingness to learn.
- Don't be afraid to ask for the skills you need.

Qualifications:

Skills:

- Define what is in it for the volunteer in terms of meeting new people, learning new skills, training, professional references, etc.
- Helping the organization is not the most powerful benefit; making a difference for the organization's beneficiaries is a key benefit.
- Think about what benefits you can offer to your volunteers that are tangible. For example, you might be able to offer gift certificates for a bookstore or coffeehouse. Training is a tangible benefit for volunteers. For example, "Training is provided on database software for all administrative volunteers."

Benefits:

PROGRESS REPORT

Vision: _____

Element	Description	Indicators and Tools	Progress, Challenges, and Needs
Resources			
Action	• Share Boomer characteristics with the Task Force and discuss strategies for creating appealing invitations to your most crucial volunteer opportunities. • Complete the Opportunities for Boomer Volunteer Engagement chart. • Complete the Boomer Volunteer Roles chart. • Complete volunteer position descriptions using our template for the Task Force and for 1–2 key volunteer positions.		
Yield			
Initial Impact			
Sustained Outcome			

4

NOTES & IDEAS

Bringing about a transformation in the actual role of older Americans will require significant cultural and institutional change. We will need to tell a new story about what is possible and desirable in later life, and to create far more compelling opportunities for translating interest into action.

—Marc Freedman, *Prime Time: How Baby Boomers Will Revolutionize Retirement and Transform America*

CHAPTER 5

Developing Connections
Networking & Cultivation

KEY CONCEPTS 🔍

1. Engaging Boomers in high-impact positions—from choosing targets to thoughtful placement—requires intentional cultivation.

2. To engage Boomers who are the best fit for your organization's culture and for the specific positions you need, you must embrace the power of the "personal ask." This can be accomplished through live interactions or electronic means.

3. A solid case statement communicates your plans and goals to important internal and external stakeholders.

In popular culture, the phrase "the Three Rs" refers to "Reading, 'Riting, and 'Rithmetic." Among traditional volunteer management professionals, the three Rs have long referred to "Recruitment, Retention, and Recognition." For decades, these three aspects of volunteer management have been the pillars of successful work with volunteers. With Boomers, that model will not work. Recruitment is an effort directed externally and aims to find and attract individuals to fit into preexisting jobs, designed by staff to serve organizational needs. Conversely, volunteer engagement focuses on volunteer cultivation. Cultivation is a broad process, directed both internally and externally, and aims to work with and develop existing and potential volunteers to find a good fit now, with significant potential for growth. Successful cultivation creates sustainable volunteer collaborations.

Today there are many ways in which a potential volunteer can begin to dialogue with a nonprofit about volunteering. These various means of initiating the dialogue are entry points or "portals" into the organization. Until recently, entering a portal was, in most cases, a two-step process. A nonprofit broadcast its messages about volunteer opportunities, most often through print and media (e.g., brochures, mailings, public service announcements), and potential volunteers had to heed that call-to-action by phoning, going to an office, or attending an event at which point they might begin a conversation about volunteering. Traditional printed collateral is one-dimensional, limited in scope, and often outdated as soon as it is printed. The Internet and other technologies are revolutionizing this part of volunteer cultivation. Portals powered by technology are multidimensional, flexible, and immediate. With technology, a volunteer can heed the call-to-action immediately by submitting information, completing an online form, or sending a query by email in just a few keystrokes. Online portals are highly effective in cultivating Boomers who are computer savvy and already rely on computers for information, communication, and connecting to others.

An organization's website is a critical tool in communicating information and resources to Boomer stakeholders. The website must be professional, up-to-date, and designed with volunteer cultivation in mind—including easy-to-use navigation and strategically placed messaging about volunteering on each page. Many nonprofits have made "donate now" buttons standard features on their websites, but make it harder for users to find ways to give of their skills and time. Effectively incorporating volunteer cultivation into website design involves creating opportunities for communication to flow in two directions. Websites should be designed not only to broadcast information about the organization and its services, but to gather information about and invite a dialogue with potential volunteers about what they are interested in and available to do.

Another portal to gather information and identify potential volunteers is a volunteer matching search engine, such as VolunteerMatch.org or Idealist.org. Web-based volunteer matching engines have emerged as a major force in volunteer recruitment and cultivation. These volunteer matching search engines can seamlessly integrate their data gathering systems and volunteer opportunity directories with a nonprofit's own homepage. This link invites existing and potential volunteers to easily and immediately learn about volunteer opportunities with the organization. Potential volunteers can—and will—click and peruse the opportunities that are appealing and match their interests and skills. Designing clear and easy navigation from the homepage is the first step, but once on the volunteer matching search engine, Boomers will engage more deeply only if the messaging about the position is attractive and convincing, utilizing, for example, pictures, questionnaires, and inspiring stories.

Volunteer matching search engines build the cultivation capacity of a nonprofit at little or no cost and do so almost immediately. Additionally, the number of people reached by web-based messaging is limitless. For example, in March 2008, VolunteerMatch boasted 3,421,609 referrals to 50,724 volunteer opportunities at 56,919 organizations.[43] Web volunteer matching search engines allow local organizations to capture the attention of volunteers in a much wider geographic area. Nonprofits that create virtual volunteer opportunities (such as research, data management, and communication) are poised to take advantage of this wider market.

As mentioned above, volunteer matching engines not only communicate the nonprofit's opportunities in an effective way, but also have the capability to gather important information about potential volunteers. By prompting for more information about skills, interests, and experience, the nonprofit can respond more easily to the potential volunteer by email, by phone, or in person. Remember to keep the time commitment requirements as flexible as possible to attract Boomer volunteers.

Prior to online networks, a person's social circles degraded as they aged, but now they can maintain and increase their social connections online.

—*Mature Interaction,* newsletter, Volume 1, Issue 3

In today's technology-driven world, the more portals or entry points created by a nonprofit, the wider their influence and success in advocacy, fund-raising, marketing, and volunteer cultivation. In addition to creating sophisticated and user-friendly navigation on their websites, agencies should invite users to volunteer on all agency collateral materials. Other strategies include phone messaging that invites callers to volunteer, a speakers' bureau of trained Boomer volunteers for outreach into their circles of influence, and stories of successful volunteer engagement on websites and newsletters. Websites that offer classified ads, like Craigslist, have also proven to be successful in generating interested volunteers.

Networking and the Personal Ask

In the past, organizations have rarely considered tapping their full circle of influence when recruiting volunteers. Instead they have relied on mass external recruitment efforts such as brochures, announcements, and mailings. When the recruitment focus is primarily external, opportunities to access the abundant resources that exist within the organization's substantial circles of influence (including donors, funders, clients and their families, partners, event participants, and vendors) are lost or underutilized. By cultivating an existing relationship, nonprofits increase the likelihood of success in recruitment efforts because the engaged individual has already demonstrated some level of commitment to the nonprofit.

For decades, the most powerful tool to cultivate an existing relationship has been the "personal ask." For Boomers, the personal ask is especially important because they are natural networkers. In the late 1960s, Boomers coined the term "networking" as part of their efforts to build powerful social and professional connections that have served them well over the years. With the epic rise of online social networking websites and other related online technologies, the concept of networking has been revolutionized because these technologies provide a means to foster and maintain existing relationships in numbers previously unimaginable.

Numerous social networking sites specifically aimed at Boomers have sprouted up over the last few years, such as Eons.com, BoomJ.com, and TBD.com. (For more sites, see the "Resources" section at the back of this guidebook.) These and other sites, such as the business networking site LinkedIn.com, serve as a digital version of the professional networking outlets spearheaded by Boomers in the late 1960s. Meanwhile, Boomers are joining existing social networking sites that were formerly the exclusive domain of young people, such as Facebook (Boomers are thought to be 40% of their subscribers[44]) and MySpace (Boomers constitute approximately half of their subscribers[45]).

Social networking enables Boomers to defy history by actually expanding their social network in retirement rather than watching it diminish, which was the experience of their Greatest Generation and Silent Generation predecessors. With the advent of social networking websites, Boomers' social networks and circles of influence expanded significantly. With the click of a mouse, a Boomer can share information about a recent volunteer experience or extend an invitation to come along on an upcoming volunteer opportunity to hundreds of people in his social circle. By posting a compelling story in her personal profile on a social networking site or listing a meaningful nonprofit affiliation on her business networking profile, a Boomer can share these messages with thousands of others in an instant. While the ever-powerful personal ask used to rely on face-to-face encounters or telephone calls, technology has transformed the personal ask to an unprecedented potential, as it can now be extended virtually through email, social networking sites, blogs, and more. Word-of-mouth efforts expand beyond one-on-one conversation to virtual conversations with large numbers of people.

The implications for nonprofits are staggering. Applying online social networking technologies to the networking-savvy men and women of the Boomer generation is a must in creating the culture of Boomer volunteer engagement. Using social networking sites is a fast, smart, effective, and immediate cultivation mechanism to engage volunteers. And it is free. From small start-up organizations to large established nonprofits, all can and should take advantage of these powerful tools to both cultivate existing volunteers and search for more volunteers.

As with every marketing strategy, online social networking is more effective if the message is clear and strategically crafted. In volunteer cultivation—whether using online social networking or traditional face-to-face networking—nonprofits must carefully craft the case statement for the work, use that as a foundation for messaging, and then strategically broadcast it. Beyond that, the process is organic and the nonprofit intentionally relinquishes control. The nonprofit can nurture and feed the strategic message, but the enterprise is dynamic when it is in the hands of the nonprofit's circle of influence.

Case statements are effective in recruitment and cultivation via electronically driven or in-person personal asks because they:

- Clearly and concisely communicate the vision and rationale behind a cause
- Highlight the needs the effort is designed to address
- Provide focus and consistency throughout the life of an initiative
- Serve as a uniform and dynamic reference for key stakeholders and spokespersons
- Function as the foundation for internal and external promotion

Full case statements usually include:

- Background on how the initiative or volunteer position came to be and why it is a strategic priority
- Brief speaking points
- An elevator speech (sound bites)
- Clear connection to organizational mission and vision
- Powerful success stories that can be leveraged
- Examples of existing exemplary programs and services within the organization
- Significant financial supporters and other powerful allies

Below is a sample case statement for Boomer volunteer engagement.

Case Statement for the Boomer Volunteer Engagement Initiative

Inspired by our mission and by the abundance of resources offered by the Boomer generation, our agency's leadership has a vision of an organizational future in which staff and volunteers work in a fully collaborative relationship to meet the immediate and long-term needs of the organization and its clients. These leaders acknowledge that effective volunteer engagement begins with an attitudinal shift—from a mindset of "never enough" to one of "abundance." By recognizing the skills and passions of individual potential volunteers and of the whole Boomer generation, the culture shifts from one of limits to one of possibilities.

To harness these possibilities, we are:

- **Developing a multitude of portals** through which thousands can engage with our organization in ways that are meaningful to them and to the organization.

- **Building an organizational structure** in which Boomer volunteer expectations are balanced with organizational needs.

- **Creating meaningful and rewarding career paths for Boomer volunteers** who will build organizational capacity, enhancing volunteer recruitment and retention.

- **Broadening and enhancing staff career paths**, thanks to the efficiency gained by increased volunteer engagement.

In other words, the Boomer Volunteer Engagement initiative is a vehicle to enable our nonprofit to expand capacity and reach its full potential through a partnership with Boomer volunteers.

Speaking Points

- Over the course of this initiative, the organization will establish itself as a learning organization in which staff and Boomer volunteers work together to develop the means to fulfill the strategic plan and advance themselves professionally.
- Effective Boomer volunteer engagement begins with an attitudinal shift—from a mindset of scarcity to one of abundance.
- Staff and Boomer volunteers at all levels of the organization are creating a dynamic exchange of wisdom, experience, and innovation to evolve the initiative from plan to action and from action to impact.
- By engaging Boomer volunteers collaboratively at all levels of the organization, staff can focus on higher-level directives, emerging initiatives, and their department's "wish list."

Elevator Speech

Our nonprofit has embarked on an initiative to engage Boomer volunteers in new and unprecedented ways. We recognize that through a truly collaborative relationship between staff and Boomer volunteers, our organization can engage thousands of Boomers and harness their skills and passions to help build the capacity of the organization. Staff and volunteers have created a partnership through the Boomer Volunteer Engagement Task Force and will:

- Pilot a number of portals through which volunteers can engage with the organization
- Create meaningful career paths for staff and volunteers
- Develop a structure that aligns Boomers' expectations with our organizational needs

In this way, we are leveraging shifting demographics to fulfill the organization's mission.

As a Task Force, develop a case statement for your Boomer Volunteer Engagement initiative, using the template on the following page.

Case Statement for Boomer Volunteer Engagement

Element	Example	Your Case Statement
Background on how initiative began and why it is a strategic priority	Inspired by research that indicates Boomers have the ability and willingness to volunteer in order to expand our resources	
Connection to organizational mission and vision	. . . to find a cure for and manage this devastating disease, our organization will engage Boomers in our efforts to support research, patient services, early detection, treatment, and education	
Financial supporters, including stakeholders and powerful allies	• We will motivate our stakeholders (staff, board, volunteers, funders, service providers, clients, and others) to join us in cultivating Boomer volunteers • We will sensitize our stakeholders to the motivations and needs of Boomer volunteers	
Examples: success stories and exemplary programs and services	We will share stories such as . . .	

Element	Example	Your Case Statement
Speaking Points	• Boomers are an abundant resource that can enable our organization to fulfill its mission of eliminating this disease. • Boomer volunteers can partner with staff to accomplish our goals. • Boomers can enlarge our organization's circle of influence in order to increase awareness, raise funds, and cultivate more volunteers.	
Elevator Speech	Our nonprofit has embarked on an initiative to engage Boomer volunteers in new and unprecedented ways. We can harness Boomers' entrepreneurial nature and sixties idealism. We can involve Boomers in every area of our organization. Together, we will transform our organization from one with too few resources to one with an abundance of human and financial resources to fight this disease.	

Once you have developed your case statement, you have a foundation from which to develop customized messages for some of your available volunteer positions. The messages and methods that bring Boomers to volunteering must be different from those that successfully attracted previous generations. Because of their unique traits and motivations, Boomers respond to messages that communicate:

- Flexibility and control over time
- Opportunities for lifelong learning
- Intergenerational experiences
- The prospect for social legacy and impact
- The prospect of utilizing their skills

Using the example of a health organization, below is one possible targeted online cultivation message you can use as a reference.

Graphic Designer
[Name of organization] is embarking on a new program initiative to bring grassroots education programs on healthy living into underserved neighborhoods, and we want a logo and graphic identity package to communicate the excitement and urgency of this initiative. We are looking for someone with graphic design and/or advertising experience who can develop a brand and graphic look for this initiative that can be incorporated into marketing and fund-raising materials to spread the word about this life-changing—and potentially lifesaving—initiative. Join a dynamic, passionate team, whether you work from home or in our office. Skills: creativity, professional graphic design skills, your own computer graphics programs and printers, the desire to help ensure a healthy future for all communities.

For other examples, peruse volunteer matching search engines to find language that matches Boomer traits and that resonates for your organization.

As you develop your customized messages for specific volunteer positions, follow these guidelines to ensure a concise and effective message. The title of the opportunity should make the prospective volunteer receptive to the opportunity and eager to learn more (see Chapter 4, "Creating the Opportunity"). The position overview should also be brief, descriptive, and compelling.

High-level volunteer opportunities should include:

- A catchy, descriptive title
- Short descriptive sentences
- A call-to-action
- No more than nine sentences: three focused on the impact of work, three describing the impact of organization, and three describing the actual tasks and time commitment

Boomer-targeted messages should avoid the words "senior," "older," and "retired," as Boomers generally do not like or relate to these terms.

Use the following template to develop messages for the position descriptions you developed in Chapter IV. Track your progress on cultivation, using the Progress Report template.

⚙️⚙️ **Messages for Position Descriptions**

Title

....

....

Call-to-Action

....

....

....

Position Overview, including three sentences on impact of work, three sentences on impact of the organization, and three sentences describing actual tasks and time commitment

....

....

....

....

....

....

....

....

....

....

....

....

PROGRESS REPORT

Vision: _____

Element	Description	Indicators and Tools	Progress, Challenges, and Needs
Resources			
Action	• Draft a case statement for your overall Boomer volunteer engagement plan. • Discuss specific case statement audiences and capture Task Force members' suggestions for audience-based additions to the case statement. • Choose the best representatives for your most important "personal asks." • Utilize online portals and social networking opportunities.		
Yield			
Initial Impact			
Sustained Outcome			

CHAPTER 6

Capitalizing on Boomer Resources

Motivational Analysis

KEY CONCEPTS 🔍

1. People have different motivational styles. Tapping into a Boomer volunteer's individual motivation increases his or her level of engagement, success, and impact in volunteering.

2. Many volunteer positions are particularly well suited for individuals with a particular motivational style; motivational styles should be considered when developing Boomer volunteer positions and cultivating individuals to fill those positions.

3. When putting together a Boomer work team, include members with varying motivational styles to strengthen the effectiveness and impact of the team's efforts.

4. Recognition and acknowledgment are more meaningful when tailored to a Boomer's particular motivational style.

All behavior is motivated. Encouraging positive behavior (like volunteering) involves identifying the right motivator to spur the action. While one Boomer volunteer may want to leave a social legacy, another may be looking for public recognition, a sense of self-validation, or a social outlet. Most people volunteer for a complex set of motivations. Tapping a volunteer's motivation will increase that person's productivity and tenure in the volunteer position. With Boomers, understanding and applying motivational theory is particularly important because Boomers' volunteerism is tied to personal motivation. This motivation is different from their Greatest Generation and Silent Generation predecessors, who volunteered for the sake of volunteering and out of a larger sense of duty to country and community, often anonymously.[46] As described in detail in Chapter 1, Boomers volunteer for personal reasons, to use their skills, and to leave a social legacy.

In her book *The Effective Management of Volunteer Programs*, Marlene Wilson refers to David C. McClelland's motivational theory, which identifies three motives that impact work behavior: achievement, power, and affiliation.[47] (Each of these motives is described more fully below.) While Boomers are diverse in their particular motivational styles as individuals, they are unique as a cohort in how strongly tied to motivation their behavior is. Boomers are motivated by personal meaning, personal relevance, and personal benefit. Matching volunteer positions to an individual Boomer's motivational style is critical. If a Boomer's volunteer position is not well matched to his or her motivational style, it is unlikely this person will stick around for long.

Achievement Volunteers

- Look for projects that have a beginning, middle, and end
- Want feedback that is clear and concrete
- Are interested in assignments in which they have the opportunity to solve problems, provide feedback, and suggest improvements
- Seek assignments that are time limited
- Want control over the results of the work
- Are interested in processes that lead to accomplishing goals and exceeding expectations

Power Volunteers

- Seek assignments that have significant and definable impact
- Desire to have influence
- Want to share their ideas
- Are interested in prestige, status, and position
- Are interested in leading processes that will make the whole organization better

Affiliation Volunteers

- Are interested in being with others
- Prioritize building friendships and relationships through work
- Desire a warm, friendly, and supportive work environment
- Demonstrate concern and caring for others
- Prioritize relationships
- Are interested in processes that strengthen the relationships that will sustain them through their engagement

When developing positions for Boomer volunteers, considering motivational styles helps broaden the spectrum of volunteer roles and attunes staff to the nuances of work that needs to get done. Most volunteer positions lend themselves to a particular motivational style. Consider the following examples of positions, organized by the motivational style with which they are most compatible.

To increase older adult activity in community service, we must first possess a better understanding of Baby Boomers, more specifically their interests and motivations.

—*Baby Boomers and the New Age of Volunteering,* Corporation for National & Community Service

Volunteer Positions Compatible with Motivational Styles

Achievement	Power	Affiliation
• Task Force Participant • Personal Trainer • Accountant • Systems Analyst • Organizational Development Consultant • Program Evaluator • Event Planner • Facilitator • Treasurer • Attorney	• Board Member • Committee Chair • Volunteer Leader • Advocate • Public Speaker • Event Manager • Fund-raiser • Project Manager • Strategic Planner • Team Leader	• Counselor • Mentor • Health Services Provider • Mediator • Crisis Intervention Specialist • Therapist • Victim Advocate • Safety Educator • Sports Coach • Tutor • Committee Member

Teams function most effectively when all motivational styles are represented. For example, a team made up exclusively of people whose chief motivator is affiliation would be a very caring group, but the work at hand might be secondary to taking care of the needs of team members. A team limited to those driven by a need for achievement could develop infighting when everyone wants to control the final product.

Volunteer Positions Compatible with Motivational Styles

Area of Work	Achievement	Power	Affiliation
Fund-raising	• Developer of fund-raising plan or media kit • Evaluator of fund-raising results	• Project manager • Spokesperson	• Planning committee member • Giving circle host
Program Delivery	• Program curriculum developer • Training evaluator	• Team leader • Program director	• Mentor • Counselor • Caregiver
Board of Directors	• Task force committee member • Audit committee member	• Board president • Executive committee member	• Membership committee member • Focus group host

Understanding motivational style will help you guide volunteers to positions they find most fulfilling, especially Boomers who want to be engaged in what is important and meaningful to them. Each individual, a Boomer or someone from another age cohort, has multiple motivations, but many people have a primary motivational style. Incentives to volunteer may change over time. Placing volunteers in positions that provide ongoing work and recognition that fit their particular motivational style or styles will be more rewarding and, ultimately, more successful for everyone. Being able to understand and leverage the motivational styles of your current and potential volunteers begins with better understanding your own style and that of your fellow Boomer Volunteer Engagement Task Force members.

At a Task Force meeting, ask all participants to complete the following motivational analysis exercise. Use the key at the end of the exercise to determine your motivational style(s). As a group, discuss everyone's responses and styles. Are there surprises? Is your Task Force balanced among different styles? How do those styles relate or not relate to the work you each have been assigned on the Task Force? Would there be a more effective distribution of work? What can you learn from the unique motivations of the Boomers on the Task Force? View this discussion as an opportunity to get to know each other better, forge more effective working relationships, and strengthen your team and the initiative as a whole. Have fun with it. There are no wrong answers!

 ## Motivational Analysis

Adapted with permission from *The Volunteer Development Toolbox: Tools and Techniques to Enhance Volunteer and Staff Effectiveness* by Gail Moore and Marilyn MacKenzie.[48]

Each of the following sets of statements offers three choices. Check the one that most closely fits your own motivations. Remember, there are no wrong answers.

1. ____a. When doing a job, I seek feedback.
   ____b. I prefer to work alone and am eager to be my own boss.
   ____c. I feel less comfortable when forced to work alone.

2. ____a. I go out of my way to make friends with new people.
   ____b. I enjoy a good argument/debate.
   ____c. After starting a task, I am not comfortable until it is completed.

3. ____a. Status symbols are important to me.

____b. I am always getting involved in group projects.

____c. I work better when there is a deadline.

4. ____a. I work best when there is some challenge involved.

____b. I would rather give orders than take them.

____c. I am sensitive to others—especially when they are angry.

5. ____a. I am eager to be my own boss.

____b. I accept responsibility eagerly.

____c. I try to develop a personal relationship with my teammates.

6. ____a. I am uncomfortable when forced to work alone.

____b. I prefer being my own boss, even when others feel a joint effort is required.

____c. When given responsibility, I set measurable standards of high performance.

7. ____a. I am very concerned about my reputation or position.

____b. I have a desire to outperform others.

____c. I am concerned with being liked and accepted.

8. ____a. I enjoy and seek warm, friendly relationships.

____b. I attempt complete involvement on a project.

____c. I want my ideas to predominate.

9. ____a. I desire unique accomplishments.

____b. I like to work with others.

____c. I have a need and desire to influence others.

10. ____a. I think about consoling and helping others.

____b. I am verbally fluent.

____c. I am restless and innovative.

11. ____a. I set goals and think about how to attain them.

____b. I think about ways to challenge people.

____c. I think a lot about my feelings and the feelings of others.

Key: Check your answers. The style with the most answers is your primary style.

1. a. Achievement
   b. Power
   c. Affiliation

2. a. Affiliation
   b. Power
   c. Achievement

3. a. Power
   b. Affiliation
   c. Achievement

4. a. Achievement
   b. Power
   c. Affiliation

5. a. Power
   b. Achievement
   c. Affiliation

6. a. Affiliation
   b. Power
   c. Achievement

7. a. Power
   b. Achievement
   c. Affiliation

8. a. Affiliation
   b. Achievement
   c. Power

9. a. Achievement
   b. Affiliation
   c. Power

10. a. Affiliation
    b. Power
    c. Achievement

11. a. Achievement
    b. Power
    c. Affiliation

Once your Task Force members have analyzed their own and each other's primary motivation styles, it is time to apply this thinking to your current volunteer pool. As a group, make a list of eight to ten current Boomer volunteers. Use the information about achievement-, power-, and affiliation-oriented volunteers to answer the following questions about each of them. We are not suggesting that you give the analysis exercise to each volunteer; rather use it as a guide for uncovering their motivations.

- What motivational style does each have?
- What can you do to support each motivational style?
- What will you do as the motivational needs of the volunteers change over time?
- How will your volunteers get a motivational paycheck for their volunteer contributions? For example, for affiliation-driven volunteers, reputation and companionship may be the reward. For achievement-driven volunteers, the payoff may be information and impact. Meanwhile, the reward for power-driven volunteers may be honor and influence.
- What types of recognition and acknowledgment are appropriate for this motivational style?

Information about the motivational styles of your volunteers will be useful in expanding their current roles and contributions to the organization. It is also critical to consider at the very start of a volunteer's relationship with your organization. Considering a potential volunteer's particular motivational style is invaluable in making an appropriate match between that individual and the volunteer position, and provides insight into tailoring support and acknowledgment strategies. These additional applications of motivational analysis are explored in the next two chapters.

PROGRESS REPORT

Vision: _____

Element	Description	Indicators and Tools	Progress, Challenges, and Needs
Resources			
Action	• Learn the motivational styles of Task Force members. • Identify gaps and balance the Task Force through invitations to additional participants as needed. • Label key volunteer position descriptions with the motivational style(s) that would enable the volunteer to be most effective.		
Yield			
Initial Impact			
Sustained Outcome			

CHAPTER 7

Creating the Collaboration

Interviewing & Finding the Fit

KEY CONCEPTS 🔍

1. A positive, professional initial contact between a potential Boomer volunteer and a nonprofit increases the chances of his or her future engagement as a volunteer because Boomers pay close attention to customer service.

2. An effective interview helps both the interviewer and the volunteer determine if the volunteer has the appropriate skills, motivational style, and fit with the organizational culture.

3. Finding a fit for a Boomer candidate is based on matching the candidate's skills, motivational style, and personality with the nonprofit's priorities and culture.

4. Customizing new position descriptions is one way to engage a talented, skilled Baby Boomer in high-level work, even if no relevant position exists.

With effective volunteer cultivation, a nonprofit should have many interested volunteers at its doorstep. What happens next is critical in successfully engaging volunteers with the organization. Nonprofits should think strategically about the Boomer's initial interface with the organization. When a Boomer is attracted enough by the carefully crafted cultivation message to call, walk in, click on the Internet portal, or go to a registration table, what is that volunteer's experience? What is the nature of that interaction? Who handles it? What information is taken? How is the interested individual moved from the "knock on the door" to an interview? Boomers are especially attuned to customer service. They evaluate the nonprofit on its responsiveness and professionalism. If they are not contacted quickly, they will find some other place to go and will tell everyone in their circle of influence about the negative experience.

Many nonprofit leaders have shared with us that having a positive first interaction makes future engagement more likely. Further, many organizations are also moving toward centralized portals by assigning a volunteer and/or staff member to serve as "gatekeeper" for the larger organization. This individual is the ambassador for the whole organization and often also serves as the initial interviewer. The gatekeeper may involve other staff or volunteers in secondary interviews with candidates who might be appropriate for their departments.

For nonprofits choosing not to centralize their entry points for volunteers, we advocate standardizing the process to ensure a level of quality control and consistency. All staff should be trained in the process: What questions do they ask the potential volunteer? What information do they take? To whom is the information forwarded? Each staff member must serve as an ambassador for the whole organization. This will ensure that a volunteer who happens initially to reach a fund-raising staff member does not end up being automatically shuttled into fund-raising committees, without consideration of the skills the individual has to offer that might better be used in program delivery, finance, or other areas of the nonprofit. We have witnessed the phenomenon of staff hoarding volunteers in their particular organizational silo. We recently saw this with a development department staff member who had identified a volunteer to recruit for fund-raisers. The volunteer was president of a large human resource professional association. It never occurred to the development worker to ask if the volunteer would share her professional skills and contacts with the whole organization.

With effective gatekeeping, potential volunteers experience the following:

- A warm, welcoming person who is interested in them and appreciates their interest in the organization
- An efficient, organized process that is standardized for all potential volunteers, no matter how they reached the "portal" (via the Internet, walking in, calling by phone, sending an email, etc.)
- An opportunity to share information about themselves, including why they are interested in volunteering, relevant experience, skills and passions, personal connection to the cause or organizational mission, and a bit about their personal life and personality
- A chance to ask questions about the organization and hear about the array of possible positions

The gatekeeper has information to share about existing volunteer positions and organizational initiatives. The gatekeeper may be the interviewer or serve as the organization's inside "connector"—identifying staff who could use the applicant's skills and experience and making the introduction between them. The gatekeeper should always follow up to ensure that communication flows between the two and the potential volunteer is not left waiting. After this initial intake is complete, the next step is the more detailed interview, designed to determine whether the match is a good one.

Interviewing: The Start of an Ongoing Dialogue

The art of screening a potential volunteer is in the gut and not in the head. Selection decisions should be based on the ideal match between what the nonprofit needs and what the volunteer wants to do and has the proficiency to do. These two statements are the keys to successful interviewing. This chapter stresses those facts and presents the fine points of power interviewing and finding a fit so that a happy, enduring relationship and ongoing dialogue are established between the nonprofit and the Boomer volunteer.

America's burgeoning older population is poised to become the new trustees of civic life in this country. These individuals have the time to care; they have the skills and experience required; they have the personal need to contribute in new ways. This match, between the untapped resources of older Americans and the needs of American communities, constitutes the great opportunity presented by America's aging.

—Marc Freedman, *Prime Time: How Baby Boomers Will Revolutionize Retirement and Transform America*

The interview creates an opportunity to identify the volunteer's priorities and lets him or her know the goals, mission, vision, and culture of the nonprofit. A good interviewer asks questions that determine the volunteer's motivational style, experience, and ability to problem solve. Successful interviews allow the volunteer's real personality to come out and help candidates decide if they fit as a volunteer. If given the opportunity, volunteers are often the best judge of whether a fit is appropriate. The interviewer can be an employee, a board member, or a volunteer. We advocate personal, one-on-one interviews, except when a large number of volunteers are needed to do the same task.

The interviewer's objective is to determine the following:

- Does the candidate have the motivation to do the work?
- Does the candidate have the skills to do the work?
- What are the candidate's expectations, and can they be met by this position?
- Will the candidate fit into the nonprofit's culture and community?

Other goals of the conversation are to:

- Encourage the candidate to communicate relevant personal information, including:
  – skills the candidate wishes to share with the nonprofit
  – goals for personal growth
  – work the candidate wishes to avoid
  – availability and schedule
- Impart the nonprofit's culture and work style
- Protect freedom of choice by giving the candidate the opportunity for choice in what he does, where he does it, and when he does it
- Determine if the recruitment program is attracting the right kind of volunteers

In our years of interviewing volunteers, we have learned a few effective tricks.

- Ask open-ended questions instead of questions that suggest the answer you are seeking or that require only a yes or no response.
- Ask unexpected questions and you will be able to observe how the candidate thinks on his/her feet.
- Allow for silences. Give the candidate time to digest what you are asking.

- Observe verbal and nonverbal cues. Assess punctuality, hygiene, and body language.
- Manage "special characters" using these techniques:
  - the rambler (the candidate who goes on and on): interrupt, redirect, or end the interview
  - the quiet one (the candidate who answers only "yes," "no," or gives very brief answers): say, "Tell me more about that," rephrase, or move on
  - the off-topic responder: repeat the question
  - the inappropriate responder: interrupt or end the interview
- Be willing to end an interview early. When you know, you know. Trust your gut.

Chapter 6 explored the importance and benefits of matching motivational style to appropriate volunteer roles. These questions and sample answers are designed to help the interviewer determine a candidate's motivational and work styles.

Motivation question: *"What are your three greatest achievements?"*

- If the greatest achievement is getting a strategic plan passed by the board of directors, the candidate is motivated by power.
- If the greatest achievement is developing the strategic plan, the candidate is motivated by achievement.
- If the greatest achievement is hosting focus groups to determine the needs to be addressed in the strategic plan, the candidate's chief motivator is affiliation.

Work style question: *"Which do you prefer and why?"*

- Volunteering with other people or working alone
  - Affiliation-motivated volunteers want to work with other people.
  - Power- and achievement-motivated volunteers may prefer working alone.

The Boomers offer this incredibly powerful window of opportunity for nonprofits to get it right in time to really harness one of the biggest resource boons the sector has seen in many decades.

—David Eisner, CEO, Corporation for National & Community Service

- Assignments with a beginning, middle, and end or ongoing assignments
  - Achievement-motivated volunteers are drawn to assignments with a clear beginning, middle, and end.
- Being an influential member of a team or assignments in which you are a leader and decision maker
  - Power-motivated volunteers like to have influence. They like to lead and make decisions. However, they appreciate working with others whom they respect, so they might like to be part of a team.
  - Affiliation-motivated volunteers want to be on teams.
  - Achievement-motivated volunteers are more interested in the results of the volunteer assignment than in the structure of the work.

Problem-solving question: Describe one of your nonprofit's initiatives and ask the candidate what she or he would do to improve it. For example, a humanitarian aid organization supports volunteer health care workers in developing countries and relies on pharmaceutical companies for medicines and medical supplies that are always in short supply. *"How can we stabilize our supply of medicines and medical supplies and have six months' reserve on hand at all times?"*

- An affiliation-motivated candidate might envision multiple auxiliaries whose members raise money or personally donate medical supplies.
- An achievement-motivated candidate might suggest a task force that would examine how similar organizations procure supplies.
- A power-motivated candidate might offer to personally go to hospital executives to solicit donations.

Situational question: This category of questions will often reveal if the candidate researched the organization, especially important for high-impact and high-visibility positions. *"Your volunteer assignment is to develop a new project for the nonprofit. What would be your first five steps? Whom would you engage to help you and why?"*

- Those who are motivated by achievement like to solve problems. This candidate might devise a well-thought-out plan with checkpoints.
- Those who are motivated by power want to share their ideas and have influence. Their steps might include reporting to the CEO or board of directors.

- Those who are motivated by affiliation are fueled by relationships. They might spend significant time describing the composition of the planning committee and how the people would drive the project.

Experiential question: *"Describe a paid or volunteer work experience in which you were the leader of other people. What went well? What didn't go well? What would you do differently next time?"*

- Candidates who stress what did not go well have low self-esteem and make poor leaders.
- Candidates who blame others for their failures are not good leaders because they fail to take responsibility and fail to support their team members.
- Candidates who have balanced responses to the question make the best leaders.

Skills question: *"What skills do you have that you are willing to share with this nonprofit if we can make it possible for you to do so?"*

- Answers to this question guide the interviewer to the best use of the candidate's skills, interests, and motivations.

Ending an interview should be done as strategically as developing the interview questions. If you believe that the match is potentially a good one, end the interview by stating that you have enjoyed the opportunity to get to know the candidate, that you recognize the many ways that he or she can contribute to the mission of the nonprofit, and suggest that each of you take some time to reflect on the possibilities and suitability of the match. Encourage him or her to really think about the position and fit. Commit to contacting the individual to follow up in a specific amount of time—twenty-four hours, three days, one week, or some other reasonable amount of time. Invite the candidate to call or email you with any questions or ideas in the meantime.

Finding the Fit

In traditional models, placement is top-down. It involves staff (or volunteer placement officers) who vet an individual for a position and put him or her into it, much like finding a square peg for a square hole. To continue the metaphor, if no square hole can be found, the volunteer is forced into a round hole or not engaged at all. But in volunteer engagement, the effort is to find—or in some cases to create—a fit. Following the interview, you have the opportunity to refer back to your position description and use the following checklist to decide whether the individual is a good match or not and whether it is worth negotiating a position customized to that individual:

- Does the candidate have the right motivational style for the assignment you are trying to fill?
- Does this individual have the skill and/or interest to do the work?
- Was the candidate punctual?
- Did the candidate ask questions? Were the candidate's questions high-quality questions, at the level you would expect of someone in the position you are offering, and articulated effectively?
- Is the candidate familiar with your organization?
- Is the candidate a fit for your organizational culture?
- Does your gut tell you that this is a person who will follow through?
- Can you work with the individual? Would you want to?

If the answers to these questions are a resounding "yes," then you have a potential match and you can begin planning your offer.

What happens when a potential volunteer emerges and offers a skill for which there is no position designed? When that occurs, consider whether that skill is aligned with organizational priorities. If there is a fit, market the volunteer to a staff or volunteer leader in the appropriate area. If the organization is interested and willing, interested parties can collaborate to design or revise an assignment that leverages the skill and helps fulfill the organization's mission. If no other appropriate opportunities exist, you can explain that there is no match at this time, but that you would like to keep him or her in mind for future opportunities.

Finally, if the individual's personality is not a good fit for the organization as a whole, you can express your appreciation for the opportunity to get to know her, explain that there are no positions that fit her qualifications, and redirect her to other organizations that might better match her skills and interests.

The Offer

If your answers to the questions above indicate a good match, you have a candidate for a volunteer position. You have both had time since the interview to think over the fit between the candidate and the position. It is time to call or meet again and make the offer. Before you ask the candidate to accept the volunteer assignment, ask:

- What questions have come up since we last spoke?
- What were your "Aha!" moments from our interview?
- What else has occurred to you over the last few days? Great ideas? Concerns?

If no surprises or red flags result from these questions, make the offer.

What if the candidate says no? Remember, stellar volunteers are not always appropriate matches for new assignments or leadership positions the organization wants them to fill. As the interviewer, you are providing:

- An easy way out before you invest more time
- A safe space for the candidate to ask questions and raise concerns that could determine success
- Another forum to learn about the candidate and his/her ideas

If the candidate opts out, ask, "May I keep you on our list for future opportunities?" Be sure to end the conversation by extending your thanks.

What if the candidate says yes? The moment the candidate accepts, your relationship enters a new level and your collaboration begins. Thank the volunteer and take a moment to allow him or her to thank you. Then state that there is a "next steps" conversation to discuss the assignment. Ask if there is a convenient time to meet by phone or in person in the next two weeks. You are creating your first agreement. The next chapter will discuss supervision and creating an Individualized Volunteer Plan.

✓ MAKING IT HAPPEN

You and your Boomer Volunteer Engagement Task Force have made great strides up to this point, working behind the scenes to reengineer your volunteer culture and publicize the opportunities through effective recruitment. Now it is time to meet the potential volunteers face-to-face. When it comes to volunteer engagement, everyone in the organization is on the front line. Every staff member and volunteer is a potential volunteer recruiter, regardless of title. Each person affiliated with the organization has family, friends, associates, and acquaintances with whom he or she speaks. Each has the potential to recruit new volunteers through personal asks or social networking. Every stakeholder might be approached by someone who is interested in volunteering. Does each staff person know how to field a question from a fellow PTA member who expresses interest in the organization? If a staff member met a man while on jury duty and heard the man express admiration for the organization's achievements, to whom would the staff member direct this person to get more information and find out how to contribute? It is important strategically to plan the process for interfacing with potential volunteers, or, as we've called it, the portal, and to share it with every staff member.

With your Task Force, create a flowchart detailing the process through which an individual moves from potential volunteer through the placement process. You can use the graphic organizer (on the facing page) as a guideline and fill it in with your organization's staff names and departments, questions to be asked, and the flow of information.

The second interview will be the one-on-one debut of your organization's new way of doing business, and this is when negotiation begins. (The next chapter will discuss negotiation in greater detail.) Before conducting interviews for your newly designed position descriptions, develop a plan, design your interview questions, and practice.

Select two or three of your new position descriptions, preferably ones that differ in the nature of the work and the type of volunteer best suited for that work. As a group or individually, brainstorm questions designed to draw out the information you need in an effective manner to make a good fit for this position. Use the Interview Questions template (page 108) and compare your ideas. How would the questions differ, if at all, for the different positions? How might candidates' answers vary, depending on their particular motivational and work styles? When do you need to ask follow-up questions? By completing templates for a few diverse positions, patterns will emerge and the Task Force members will be able to identify what types of questions and information are consistently most important to them. You will then be able to go through the process as a full team for only the most critical new positions and initiatives.

1. **Volunteer** candidate contacts organization.

2. **Organizational representative** is welcoming and appreciative. The representative learns a little about the individual, and directs him/her to the "gatekeeper."

3. **Organizational representative** forwards information to the **gatekeeper** to give a "heads up" that this individual will be calling. Ideally, the information includes candidate contact information so the gatekeeper can proactively contact the individual.

4. **Gatekeeper** conducts initial intake conversation to gather information about the individual's skills, abilities, past experience, desires, and availability.

5. Gatekeeper determines whether staff members whose needs match the potential volunteer's skills and availability should proceed with the interview process or if the gatekeeper should conduct the initial interview.

6.a Gatekeeper conducts the interview with the volunteer and determines whether the individual is a potential fit.

6.b Staff members conduct the initial interview and/or the second interview with the volunteer and determine whether the individual is a potential fit.

NO
FIT

FIT

NO
FIT

1. Problem-Solving Question

Example: Describe one of your nonprofit's initiatives and ask the candidate what she or he would do to improve it.

2. Situational Question

Example: Your volunteer assignment is to develop a new project for the nonprofit. What would be your first five steps? Whom would you engage to help you, and why?

3. Experiential Question

Example: Describe a paid or volunteer work experience in which you were the leader of other people. What went well? What didn't go well? What would you do differently next time?

4. Skills Question

Example: What are the skills at which you are proficient that you are willing to share with this nonprofit, if we can make it possible for you to do so?

Once you have developed your interview questions, practice interviewing with other team members or existing volunteers who are willing to support the initiative and perhaps become interviewers themselves.

PROGRESS REPORT

Vision: _____

Element	Description	Indicators and Tools	Progress, Challenges, and Needs
Resources			
Action	• Prepare an interview script for all positions, with a few additional questions for your highest-level volunteer positions. • Decide whether current volunteer leaders—or volunteers you develop into leaders—will conduct volunteer interviews. • Train volunteers and all staff on Volunteer Position Description template toward eventual conversion of most volunteer positions to results-based work. • Train all interviewers on interview conversation script. • Identify existing gatekeepers, and empower them to create an intake process that works for all intake portals and allows Boomer candidates to ask questions and offer additional skills.		
Yield			
Initial Impact			
Sustained Outcome			

CHAPTER 8

Nurturing the Relationship

Support

KEY CONCEPTS 🔍

1. Volunteer engagement professionals empower their volunteers.

2. Boomer volunteers seek support for their work, not supervision. They want collegial relationships with staff.

3. By negotiating, the Boomer volunteer and staff partners come to agreement on accountability, timeline, communication, outcomes, and milestone.

4. Acknowledgment is the expression of mutual appreciation and gratitude for volunteer efforts and can be achieved in innovative ways that motivate and inspire both staff and Boomer volunteers.

5. An Individual Volunteer Plan is a tool to cultivate Boomer volunteers more deeply and sustain their engagement with the nonprofit.

The moment that a volunteer accepts your invitation to take on a volunteer position, your support for him or her begins. In volunteer management models, staff members delegate tasks to volunteers and supervise their work. In volunteer engagement, staff and volunteers negotiate their work and support of each other. Traditional volunteer managers direct the work of their organizational volunteers; volunteer engagement professionals empower their volunteers to do the work of the organization. The volunteer engagement model is the only approach that resonates with Boomers' desire for autonomy, authority, impact, and opportunities to be creative and innovative. They want to be supported instead of supervised because they expect to take responsibility for their work. They don't want a boss; they want a colleague.

Negotiation

The first step in establishing a collegial relationship is the negotiation. The goal of the negotiation is mutual understanding and agreement on the following:

- Accountability: Who is accountable for what?
- Timeline: By when?
- Communication: How will information and progress be shared?
- Outcome: What will be the impact of the work?
- Milestones: At what points will progress be benchmarked and checked?

What is excluded from the negotiation is the way in which the work is done. Using the Work Plan template introduced in Chapter 3, staff and volunteers must agree upon vision, resources, yield, impact, and outcome of the work. However, the way in which these outcomes are reached—the "Actions" section of the template—is up to the volunteer who is empowered to do the job. As long as the work is achieved without violating organizational policies, the volunteer can use his or her skills, ingenuity, and circles of influence to bring about the agreed-upon outcomes.

After negotiation, you are faced with the challenge and joy of living out the collaborative relationship you have just negotiated. To ensure a continued high-functioning collaboration, you must embrace volunteer engagement in all areas of support, including the evolving role of the volunteer, oversight and evaluation, and communication and hierarchy. The ultimate challenge of engaging Boomers is transforming the staff role from volunteer manager to volunteer engagement professional. The following chart illuminates some of the nuances that distinguish traditional management from collaborative engagement in terms of ongoing support of volunteers. When planning for such support, staff members need to consider the following questions:

1. If I am to engage rather than manage, what do I need to change about how I support the volunteer?
2. What new support might I need? Training? Support from my supervisor? A coach?
3. If I supervise employees, how will I manage employees in this new culture? How will I hold them accountable for collaborative engagement?

With those questions in mind, review the following chart and consider how you will steer your nonprofit as it evolves toward a culture of volunteer engagement.

Volunteer Engagement

Volunteer Management	Differ In	Volunteer Engagement
Position centered; static	◄ Volunteer Role ►	People / skill based; dynamic
The numbers and logistics	◄ Recruitment Focus ►	The vision to be met
Organizational need	◄ Alignment ►	Synergy between organizational need and volunteer proficiencies
Volunteer manager controls top-down, staff-driven work; responsibility rests with, and success depends on, that staff person	◄ Oversight and Communication ►	Volunteer engagement employs a transparent process with strategic focus on results; responsibility rests with everyone; success depends on collaboration
Volunteer performance	◄ Evaluation Focus ►	Impact of volunteer effort
Volunteer as subordinate	◄ Hierarchy ►	Volunteer as colleague
Recruitment	◄ Placement ►	Cultivation

Sustainable, Ongoing Engagement

In the last line of the preceding chart, "recruitment" vs. "cultivation" is a key concept in retaining Boomer volunteers. Boomers want a supportive, collaborative relationship that nurtures their talents and skills and helps them thrive as volunteers. In volunteer management models, recruitment is what gets volunteers in the door. In volunteer engagement, cultivation is the process that not only gets them in the door, but keeps them moving forward into new and often deeper engagement with the organization. For Boomers, the opportunity to grow in the position is essential to keeping them engaged and should be built into the "Staff Support" section of all agreements.

First, consider whether your position-based retention plans incorporate the three motivational styles from Chapter 6. If someone's motivation is:

Achievement: Give more and varied opportunities with increasing responsibility. Avoid boredom and bear in mind that repetition diminishes impact and fulfillment. She is most likely to stay with the project or position if her role is integral to getting the work done well and exceeding expectations.

Power: Give more power, influence, access, and leadership roles. He enjoys seeing the big picture and is most likely to stay with the project or position if his role is integral to leading it.

Affiliation: Give opportunities to meet more people and create community in the team. She is most likely to stay with the project or position if her role is integral to maintaining the relationships that enable the work to get done together.

Volunteer Decision Making and Leadership

Another way to cultivate, deepen, and sustain the involvement of Boomers is to give them responsibility for decision making in their work. Greatest Generation and Silent Generation volunteers were often content with little or no responsibility for decision making. Boomers and the generations that follow expect to have the ability to make decisions about the direction, pace, and process of work they are doing. They are more than willing to collaborate with staff and other volunteers to accomplish the goals for their work. However they chafe—or walk away—when all of the work is directed by staff. In order for an organization to fully embrace capacity building through volunteer engagement, staff and board members must be ready and willing to share decision-making responsibility.

In our work we have encountered many staff members who have concern about volunteers' ability to take on and manage full decision-making authority. We contend that when the result of volunteer engagement is clearly articulated and boundaries are established, volunteers are fully capable of making decisions that fit with impact, outcome, strategic priorities, and mission. Rising to a higher level of expectation, volunteers find more satisfaction from their work and their ability to make an impact as a result of their work. Many Boomer volunteers will see more authority as a goal to strive for during their volunteer experience—even as a promotion.

As you cultivate Boomer volunteers, you build trust and understanding. You develop a picture of what the volunteer can and cannot handle. You would not and should not give volunteers total responsibility in the beginning of their relationship with your nonprofit. As trust deepens, the project leader (staff or volunteer) knows when to add and when not to add decision making to the volunteer's responsibilities, or even if this move to a higher level of responsibility is appropriate. Decision making is not an all-or-nothing proposition. Volunteers might have responsibility in one area and not in others. For example, the volunteer does not decide on the budget for event expenses but can decide how to spend specific line items or the full allocated amount.

Volunteers who present challenges are not likely candidates to move along this continuum. If you have a "problem volunteer" who is struggling with decision-making authority, provide coaching and support. Make sure that you have a solid relationship before you begin to vet the volunteer for more authority.

Just as they [Boomers] will not be attracted to many of the traditional volunteer assignments, they will also balk at management systems that do not recognize their personal levels of competence and expertise.

—Mary Merrill, "New Research on Boomers and Retirement," www.merrillassociates.net

Here are some tips to know when a volunteer is ready for more:

- The volunteer demonstrates commitment and follow-through in work assignments.
- The volunteer requests to do more.
- The project leader (staff member or another volunteer) sees signs that the volunteer is capable of more.
- The project leader sees evidence of ability from observing the volunteer's problem-solving capability.
- The project leader identifies the volunteer as someone who sees the big picture, understands organizational priorities and politics, and has the communication skills to provide feedback on his or her progress.

There is both art and science to the process of empowering volunteers. If you are not sure whether a volunteer is ready for more, partner the volunteer with a trusted coleader of a task force first and observe that veteran and the team's response. Evaluate the program's success and ask the volunteer about her or his personal contributions. That shadowing experience gives your established leader assistance and a powerful role, shaping a future leader or perhaps a successor.

Ultimately, determinations about volunteer decision-making and leadership are defined and negotiated by answering the following questions:

- What is the scope of decision-making authority for the volunteer in this position?
- To whom will the volunteer report decisions about this project? In what time frame?
- What is the mechanism to discuss these decisions when they are correct and when they may be incorrect?
- How will you share the impact of the decisions with the volunteer?
- What risks are the volunteer and the organization willing to take?

It is a solid investment to choose to cultivate a Boomer volunteer leader over sufficient time to gain trust that he or she will not let you down. In addition to increasing your own capacity, that leader is likely to engage other Boomer volunteers effectively.

Often, thoughtfully increased autonomy leads to a greater sense of ownership, which in turn yields solidly organized efforts. Boomer volunteers expect clearly defined responsibilities, competent financial management, and productive meetings with agendas that allow for discussion while maintaining focus. Moreover, a volunteer leader who is gradually promoted to a high degree of "ownership" knows the project's needs well enough to offer the flexibility Boomer volunteers demand.

Perhaps the most important reason to carefully cultivate powerful Boomer volunteer leaders—such as event and task force chairs—is to ensure deepening engagement of the other volunteers they will lead: the workers and task force members who consistently achieve your organization's goals. Boomer volunteers, after they have volunteered once or twice, will look at who is leading before they say yes. "Yes" will be the answer much more frequently if they have experienced your volunteer leader(s) listening well, motivating and meaningfully acknowledging team members, and clearly articulating and achieving goals.

Acknowledgment

All volunteers must be cultivated through acknowledgment of their efforts and contributions. Acknowledgment includes recognition for work and sharing gratitude and appreciation for the personal contributions the volunteer has made. In traditional volunteer management models, recognition is something staff give to volunteers and is primarily event based. Pins, plaques, and awards meant a lot to Silent Generation and Greatest Generation volunteers. Boomers and subsequent generations stay away from recognition events and do not want a pin or plaque. Most will not wear the pin or display the plaque, and many object to the nonprofit spending money on them. While the old recognition strategies and events have their value, they can no longer be the sole focus of recognition.

Acknowledgment can be made by staff for volunteers, by volunteers for staff, and by volunteers for other volunteers. Acknowledgment can occur in innovative and truly meaningful ways. For an achievement-motivated Boomer volunteer who reaches a benchmark in a lengthy project, what better acknowledgment than to have the staff and volunteer partners invited to lunch with the CEO to share their progress and ideas for project

Volunteers, we know, have to get more satisfaction from their work than paid employees, precisely because they do not get a paycheck. They need, above all, challenge. They need to know the organization's mission and to believe in it. They need continuous training. They need to see results.

—Peter Drucker, *Management Challenges for the 21st Century*

improvement? That same lunch would be appropriate for a power-motivated volunteer who likes to converse about ideas with people of influence. And the affiliation-motivated volunteer would appreciate the lunch because it provides a venue for socializing.

We have found that using motivational analysis as your guide will inspire new and creative ideas about acknowledgment. If someone's motivation is:

Achievement: Share what happened because of his work. Acknowledge his unique contributions and skills. Provide opportunities for additional challenge and high-level interaction. For example, give formal recognition by board or team leadership, resources for specific training and development, and opportunities to present findings, evaluate results, and make recommendations to decision makers.

Power: Provide opportunities for upward mobility, decision making, strategic thinking, and influencing direction. For example, promote to positions of authority or positions with access to authority. Recognize publicly for leadership; consider public honors, like naming a room or a fund.

Affiliation: Recognize in group settings and "break bread" together. Express gratitude often. Acknowledge life cycles. For example, hold a team potluck on the anniversary of her first day of volunteering. "Warm fuzzies" and frequent thank-you notes from the team leaders are also important.

Here are a few ideas for Boomer-friendly acknowledgment:

- Offer opportunities for professional development, such as increasingly interesting and important volunteer positions, management training and leadership development seminars, access to organizational research, and mentoring and coaching opportunities.
- Demonstrate respect for the volunteers' time by negotiating deadlines, providing opportunities to cycle in and out of volunteering, and offering flexibility in where, when, and especially how the job is done.
- Encourage input and feedback on the nonprofit's operations.
- Provide adequate resources for volunteers to be successful, such as training, human resources, technology, budget, and work space.

- Provide a new option each year for volunteers to select, such as a gift or gift certificates (from bookstores, coffee retailers, movie theaters), tickets to community events, or participation in the nonprofit's events. The more choices, the better.
- Send letters of appreciation or recognition to employers and family members. This type of recognition is underutilized and can make a big difference for volunteers at low cost to the nonprofit.
- Celebrate in the community with public recognition. (Events are still viable recognition tactics if they are paired with other personalized recognition efforts.)
- Have volunteer leaders report to board and staff meetings on the results of their work.
- Feature volunteer success stories in the newsletter and local paper, on the website, in annual reports, and at nonprofit events.
- Invite volunteers to attend staff development sessions and conferences.
- Hold forums during which volunteers teach other volunteers and staff what they learn at conferences and through their work.
- Send an annual "valuation" card to high-performing volunteers from their staff partners and/or from the family or client whom they have impacted. A valuation letter is a personalized note to volunteers highlighting all the things they are currently doing well. A valuation letter reinforces the behaviors that supervisors want to cultivate and captures the essence of the volunteers' motivation.
- Include volunteers' names on a recognition plaque at the headquarters of a large organization.
- Remember, it is often the little things that convey appreciation to volunteers: coffee with staff or nonprofit executive, remembering life-cycle events in the volunteers' lives, and giving sincere thanks along the way.

✔ MAKING IT HAPPEN

Your Task Force has assessed the current state of volunteer engagement in your organization, identified needs, brainstormed opportunities, developed exciting effective ways to broadcast those positions, and designed plans to make the best match for those positions. Now it is time to contemplate how you already recognize volunteers—and to plan for new, expanded ways to provide meaningful recognition to your Boomer volunteers. As a group, complete the following exercise by filling in the column on the right, including all current recognition practices and suggestions for new ones that would effectively recognize the work of Boomer volunteers.

⚙⚙ Acknowledgment Tailored to Motivation

Motivation	Characteristics	Acknowledgment
Achievement	• Look for projects with a beginning, middle, and end • Want clear, concrete feedback • Are interested in assignments with the opportunity to solve problems • Seek assignments that are time limited • Want control over the outcome of the work	1. Attend a seminar that addresses the volunteer's assignment 2._____ 3._____ 4._____
Power	• Seek assignments with significant and definable impact • Desire to have influence • Want to share their ideas • Are interested in prestige, status, and position	1. Opportunity to report results of volunteer work to the staff and board 2._____ 3._____ 4._____
Affiliation	• Are interested in being with others • Friendship and relationships are a top priority • Desire a warm, friendly, and supportive work environment • Demonstrate concern and caring for others • Relationships may be more important than the work itself	1. Support session over coffee or lunch 2._____ 3._____ 4._____

Individual Volunteer Plan (IVP)

Volunteer support, acknowledgment, and sustainable ongoing engagement are intertwined when approached strategically. Sustaining Boomer volunteers as a resource is built on the foundation of supporting volunteers in their career development within the nonprofit organization and aligning volunteers' personal aspirations with those of the organization. Traditional recognition events (banquets) and rewards (pins, certificates) are not likely to retain the best and brightest talent. It is not enough to update your events or awards, though there is often value in doing so. You must actively cultivate top performers.

The Individual Volunteer Plan (IVP) is our adaptation of an existing tool used in related fields: the IEP, or Individual Education Plan. The purpose of the IEP is to customize learning opportunities for a student in order to help him or her achieve the best academic and behavioral results. We have applied this methodology to retaining an organization's highest-performing volunteers.

The Individual Volunteer Plan is a practical, collaborative tool developed by Jill Friedman Fixler and colleague Jennifer Rackow.[49] It shares a focus on results with the Work Plan, and opens communication between key staff members and volunteers. For Boomers, the IVP is a perfect tool to address many of their unique desires surrounding volunteerism. For the Boomer who wants meaningful work with definable impact, an IVP can be written to promise increasing impact over the volunteer's career. For the Boomer who has skills to share and values the acquisition of new skills, an IVP may offer a future of professional development and increased responsibility. For the Boomer who seeks flexibility to fit a semi-retired lifestyle, an IVP may give the volunteer a stake in planning seasonal work with the promise that the position will be there upon his or her return.

The most significant benefit of using an IVP is that the process of designing the tools strategically and intentionally develops potential staff members, board members, and volunteer leaders from your community of volunteers—people who will take your organization into your preferred future. Individual Volunteer Plans create:

- A collaborative work environment
- Clear paths of leadership, responsibility, and/or service with career paths for volunteers to follow as they serve
- Clear progression of levels of decision making within that leadership path
- Opportunities for cross-training, mentoring, coaching, and for volunteers to lead other volunteers

- New possibilities for those who have a terrific volunteer history but seem to be losing interest, decreasing commitment, or verging on problematic behavior
- A culture that is asset oriented rather than problem oriented, where you uncover volunteers' motivations and skills first and then find needs they could address
- A sophisticated way to celebrate the value of volunteer contribution

This tool is not for everyone. The reasons to design an IVP with someone are:

- You have identified this person as someone who can add value to the organization beyond what he or she is currently doing.
- The volunteer wishes to broaden and deepen his or her experience with the organization.
- You have identified that there is potential for further cultivation in role, skills, and impact.

These three qualifiers absolutely demand that you or someone you trust have experience with this individual. If you are the gatekeeper or overseer of volunteer engagement for your nonprofit, you are likely in a good position to see candidates surface. However, you need to ask staff members and other volunteers regularly, "Who is amazing?" You are, in fact, looking for your "rock star" volunteers.

Consider your pool of volunteers and generate a list of specific volunteers who might benefit from an Individual Volunteer Plan. Next, use this form to develop IVPs with those individuals. We recommend that each member of the Task Force identify two volunteers in particular who would benefit from the IVP and cowrite a plan with each of them (you can always opt to develop more or fewer, depending on the size of your nonprofit). Remember to plan for continued communication and check in on progress.

Individual Volunteer Plan (IVP)

Volunteer's Name: _____ Date: _____

Support Liaison (Supervisor): _____

Current Competencies: Baseline assessment of the volunteer's current knowledge, abilities, functioning, and accomplishments across core competencies that you or your organization has identified.

1. Communication

2. Team Building and Collaboration

3. Technology Acumen

4. _____

5. _____

6. _____

Goals and Benchmarks: Once you are both clear on the volunteer's current level of performance, you can—together—choose skills, competencies, and experiences on which to focus. For each focus area, set a goal and some benchmarks along the way so that you can both assess progress toward each goal.

This is a great place to use Work Plan thinking—with a twist:

• Start with the vision you share for this volunteer's role in your organization. Get specific and make sure the vision inspires the volunteer and meets the needs of the volunteer and your organization.

• What resources do you need? Consider training, time, and money. Then, reverse your thinking. What resources will you now have because of this volunteer's progress? That answer will lead you directly to results.

- What will happen as a result of this person's success? What will change, in the short and long term, for this volunteer? For the volunteer program? For the community? For your organization? For the specific strategic objective this volunteer is going to steward or fulfill?

1. _____

2. _____

3. _____

4. _____

5. _____

6. _____

Additional Needs: This is the place to add services or equipment this volunteer will need to reach the goals you have chosen successfully. These services could include specific items like special software, assistive devices and other accommodations, and general requests such as transportation and training.

1. _____

2. _____

3. _____

4. _____

5. _____

6. _____

Signatures: While many volunteer position agreements have a place where volunteers sign to indicate they will abide by organizational regulations and they understand their commitments, signatures are rarely used—or even considered—strategically. An example of using signatures beyond risk management is using them to denote the importance of the position. A volunteer receives a very clear message when the IVP requires a signature from, for example, an Executive Director or Board President.

Volunteer: _____

Supporter (Supervisor): _____

Executive Director: _____

Board Chair: _____

Updates: We strongly recommend scheduling times when you, the volunteer, and other involved staff and volunteers convene to review progress and revise the plan as needed. However, when and how often you do this may vary, especially if you are looking at some episodic or project-based assignments and some long-term positions, or both. Find the junctures that make sense for the position and your organizational culture. For example, choose the anniversary of the person's service or a significant project completion. Also, observe the volunteer or speak to your colleagues who work with her or him to assess the need for a check-in. Strategic opportunities may also present optimal times for an update—and not just during official strategic planning. Perhaps your organization receives a sizable new gift that takes you in a new direction. Which of your top performers might be ready to step up and champion that new direction?

Date for Next Progress Review: _____

PROGRESS REPORT

Vision: _____

Element	Description	Indicators and Tools	Progress, Challenges, and Needs
Resources			
Action	• Practice having conversations to offer and negotiate key volunteer positions. • Choose appropriate starting levels of decision making for groups of volunteer positions. • Write an Individual Volunteer Plan for 1–2 key volunteer leadership positions. • Infuse volunteer acknowledgment with experiences that will resonate with people of each motivational style.		
Yield			
Initial Impact			
Sustained Outcome			

8

NOTES & IDEAS

. . . how Baby Boomers think is just as important as what they think.

—Coming of Age Incorporated

CHAPTER 9

Sustaining the Collaboration

Ongoing Engagement

KEY CONCEPTS 🔍

1. Successful Boomer volunteer engagement pilot programs can be replicated to institutionalize the initiative and build the organization's capacity.

2. The steps to maintaining a sustainable Boomer volunteer engagement model are:

   a. Measure feedback and progress

   b. Identify your champions

   c. Share your stories

   d. Dialogue

   e. Inspire others

You have just mapped out your organization's journey from volunteer management to a culture in which you will successfully engage Baby Boomers to build organizational capacity and increase nonprofit impact and outcome.

The first Boomers reached age 62 in 2008. Boomers are actively imagining their next act. Many of them see a future that involves both volunteering and employment. The Corporation for National & Community Service recently reported that Boomers are increasingly seeking to volunteer their professional skills before retirement and that this trend is likely to continue.[50] Further, the 2007 Deloitte/Points of Light study reports the following:

> Nonprofits are addressing key social and economic issues, but they often need help to achieve sustainability and large-scale impact. A 2006 impact study by Deloitte/Points of Light showed that 89% of nonprofit leaders realize that volunteers' workplace skills are extremely or very valuable to their organizations, and 77% agree that their organizations could benefit significantly from corporate volunteers focusing on business practices improvements. However, nearly two-thirds of nonprofits do not partner with any companies that provide volunteers.[51]

By inviting Boomers to partner with our organizations in ways that fit their busy lifestyles and utilize their skills, we can help them build a future that involves nonprofits and the missions we serve. If, on the other hand, we continue to operate nonprofit business as usual by managing volunteers, our opportunity diminishes significantly. We must resist the temptation simply to try harder doing business as we always have, and instead make substantive changes in the way we engage volunteers. If we do not, Boomers' attention will shift elsewhere. Nonprofit organizations offer a powerful social legacy to those who, when young, were ready to change the world. Now they have the wisdom and the skills to do it and we have the vehicles through which they can do it: our mission-driven nonprofit organizations. Moreover, when we successfully engage Boomers, we increase the opportunity to engage their Generation X and Millennial children and grandchildren as well.

It is not more work—it is different work. The time to act is now.

✅ MAKING IT HAPPEN

Using this guidebook, you and your Task Force have established a team and worked through a process in which discrete groups within your organization (your pilots) made incremental changes to engage Boomers with you as partners. You have established new practices and innovated in exciting ways. This is not the end; it is the beginning of spreading that culture of innovation, replicating the process in ever-widening circles throughout the organization. What are the next steps for you to take in order to institutionalize these volunteer engagement practices?

1. Measure Feedback and Performance

Take the feedback from your Work Plan and Progress Reports and use it to improve the pilot initiatives. Compile all of your Progress Reports and analyze them against your original plan. What have you learned along the way that will be helpful to your nonprofit in replicating your accomplishments throughout the organization? What will you do differently moving forward? What quality improvements will you implement now? Whom else can you engage to move the pilot to the next phase? Who in your circle of influence can connect you to the people you need?

2. Identify Your Champions

Identify your Boomer volunteer engagement champions. Who from your board, staff, and existing volunteers has embraced the concept of collaboration with Boomer volunteers? How can you utilize these individuals to spread the practices further within your organization? How are you rewarding them for their efforts in this regard?

3. Share Your Stories

Create an internal public relations plan about the pilot and its results. Who needs to know? What do they need to know? How and when do they need to know it? What powerful stories can you tell about the impact and outcome of Boomer volunteer

America's burgeoning older population is poised to become the new trustees of civic life in this country. These individuals have the time to care; they have the skills and experience required; they have the personal need to contribute in new ways. This match, between the untapped resources of older Americans and the needs of American communities, constitutes the great opportunity presented by America's aging.

—Marc Freedman, *Prime Time: How Baby Boomers Will Revolutionize Retirement and Transform America*

engagement? Who should be the ones to tell these stories? How and where will the team capture tools, timelines, Work Plans, and Progress Reports for others to access?

4. Dialogue

Engage the board, staff, and volunteer innovators for Boomer volunteer engagement in ongoing conversations about best practices. There are many ways to accomplish this: live meetings, video conferencing, listservs, and online social networking sites. What are they learning? What else do they need to know? What conversations should they have to replicate what they have learned? How can they continue to innovate together?

5. Inspire Others

Share what you are doing with all of your internal and external stakeholders. Sharing the results of your Boomer volunteer engagement strategy will inspire others to serve and donate to the nonprofit. Your organization will be seen as innovative and cutting-edge (which appeals greatly to Boomers and the cohorts that follow) and your access to resources will increase.

Conclusion

We have just described the continuous cycle of quality improvement of Boomer volunteer engagement practices. You align what you are doing to organizational priorities and directives. You create a Boomer volunteer engagement Work Plan to move forward. You implement the Work Plan, perhaps through a pilot initiative. You evaluate the results and measure what you did against anticipated results. You adjust based on what you have learned and begin again to improve the pilot and/or replicate what you have learned in other areas of your organization. The key is to engage Boomers in the process, as this is the meaningful work that many Boomers want to do. By asking them to create both the questions and the answers, together you cultivate shared ownership for the results and expand organizational capacity beyond the limitations of staff size and staff knowledge.

Boomer volunteer engagement is a new way of thinking. We passionately believe that this philosophy applies to the Boomer cohort and to the generations that follow.

Boomers are leading the change to more active participation in all aspects of nonprofit organizational life, which, if widely adopted, will sustain nonprofits for decades to come. While some nonprofit executives and staff worry about giving up control, we believe they will gain more in the process of Boomer volunteer engagement than they will ever lose. The result is negotiated, the relationships are collegial and collaborative, and the outcome is organizational capacity building. Meaningful work will consistently yield desired results. Be bold in what you can imagine as resources for your organization. Within your circle of influence and by accessing the abundant skills of the Boomer cohort and beyond, you have everything you will ever need.

We are optimistic about the future of volunteer engagement and see the 78.2 million Boomers as our entree into a new world where volunteers and staff collaborate to build organizational capacity and fulfill their ambitious vision and missions.

*We wish you the very best
on this important journey.*

The Boomers offer this incredibly powerful window of opportunity for nonprofits to get it right in time to really harness one of the biggest resource boons the sector has seen in many decades.

—David Eisner, CEO,
Corporation for National &
Community Service

Appendix

Downloadable PDFs are available at www.BoomerVolunteerEngagement.org

1. Make a list of people already in your circle of influence from your board, current volunteers, donors, clients and their families, partners, and vendors to invite into the planning and implementation process.

2. Of those individuals, whom would you describe as "visionary"? (Who has indicated an appreciation and understanding of the potential of Boomer volunteer engagement?)

3. Of those individuals, who are the strongest Connectors? (Who knows a lot of people? Is skilled at bringing people together? Has an extensive list of contacts and uses it?)

4. Of the individuals, who are the clear Mavens? (Which individuals have information about a topic of importance to this Task Force? Who collects information and likes to share it?)

5. Who from your list are the Salespeople? (Who is charismatic? Who is a persuader?)

6. What are the specific skills necessary for an effective Task Force for your organization? Who possesses this expertise and these talents?

YOU . . .	Score 1 if you . . .	Score 2 if you . . .	Score 3 if you . . .
Organizational Support for Volunteers			
Involve volunteers in all aspects of organizational life.	Have staff and/or a few dedicated volunteers do most of the work.	Have a volunteer presence in all aspects of organizational activities and programming.	Mandate that staff and leadership utilize volunteers in their work.
Allocate resources, including budget, space, and tools, for volunteer engagement.	Assume that volunteers are "free" and do not require resources.	Have a budget for volunteer resources.	Reflect in your annual budget detailed expenses for volunteers, including supplies, space, software, training, recruitment, staff time, and recognition.
Train staff and board leadership to work effectively with volunteers.	Assume staff and key leadership know how to work with volunteers.	Reflect responsibility for volunteer engagement in staff and lay leadership position descriptions.	Provide formal training to staff and lay leadership on how to work with volunteers.
Needs Assessment and Program Planning			
Have defined why volunteers are a strategic priority for the organization.	Use volunteers for activities and programs as they are needed.	Have identified volunteers as leaders and helpers in moving the organization forward.	Have a written philosophy statement about volunteer engagement that identifies volunteers as an indispensable channel for ideas on organizational direction and operations, programs, and activities.
Include volunteer engagement in risk management planning.	Do not consider volunteer assignments in your risk assessment.	Evaluate all volunteer assignments for risk.	Have appropriate insurance for volunteer engagement and evaluate/update as necessary.

YOU . . .	Score 1 if you . . .	Score 2 if you . . .	Score 3 if you . . .

Effective Recruitment and Cultivation

YOU . . .	Score 1 if you . . .	Score 2 if you . . .	Score 3 if you . . .
Have written position descriptions for all volunteer assignments.	Verbally explain to volunteers what they are going to do.	Have a position description for each volunteer assignment.	Conduct an annual (at minimum) review and update of all position descriptions.
Have a process for volunteer cultivation.	Do recruitment exclusively through announcements in the newsletter, website postings, etc.	Figure out who knows prospective volunteers and have them do the recruiting.	Have a written strategic recruitment plan for all volunteer assignments and needs.
Maintain current and accurate records on volunteers.	Do not track volunteer involvement.	Have a record of all volunteers and what they do for the organization.	Integrate volunteer records with membership and donor information.

Interviewing and Placement

YOU . . .	Score 1 if you . . .	Score 2 if you . . .	Score 3 if you . . .
Design volunteer assignments for a wide range of skills, ages, and interests.	Rely on a specific group of volunteers (e.g., stay-at-home mothers, retired, etc.) to get the work done.	Include all age groups and demographics among your volunteers.	Design assignments specifically to reflect a wide range of skills and interests and not limit work to clerical and administrative positions.
Screen and place volunteers in assignments that are right for them and the organization.	Let anyone volunteer for anything.	Match volunteers to the assignment that aligns with their interests.	Recruit volunteers based on their preferences, the skills they willingly share, and the relevant qualifications for the job.

Orientation and Planning

YOU . . .	Score 1 if you . . .	Score 2 if you . . .	Score 3 if you . . .
Have written policies and procedures for volunteer engagement.	Assume that volunteers know what is acceptable for them to do.	Have some policies that relate to volunteer involvement.	Have detailed written policies and procedures and orient all volunteers to these guidelines.

YOU . . .	Score 1 if you . . .	Score 2 if you . . .	Score 3 if you . . .
Supervision and Support			
Hold volunteers accountable for what they do.	Cannot fire a volunteer.	Clarify for volunteers the limits and boundaries of their assignments.	Have staff and leadership follow up with volunteers to make sure they accomplish what they set out to do, releasing them as needed.
Actively solicit volunteer input in decisions that affect them.	Have volunteers do whatever they are assigned.	Encourage current volunteers to give feedback.	Have a system in place for collecting and reflecting on volunteer feedback on decisions that affect them.
Strategies for Sustainability (Retention)			
Have volunteer assignments that are meaningful and that impact the ability of the organization to achieve its mission.	Design volunteer assignments around having people do the work of the staff and/or board of directors.	Design volunteer assignments to have an impact on the mission of the organization.	Reflect a diversity of work in volunteer assignments, from direct service to program delivery, and incorporate high-level assignments, such as the provision of professional services.
Ensure that staff and leadership recognize volunteers informally and formally.	Host an annual recognition event for volunteers.	Give frequent recognition to volunteers from the board, staff, and other volunteer leaders.	Acknowledge the successes of volunteer endeavors in personalized ways through sharing celebratory information in collateral materials (e.g., the website, newsletters, announcements, emails, and written materials), through letters, and through customized networking opportunities with organizational leaders and others.

To score your answers, see page 37.

1. What are the dreams for your organization that require more people, expertise, money, or tools to accomplish?

2. What are the problems and challenges that your organization is currently experiencing?

3. What is your nonprofit currently doing that you would like to increase, replicate, or expand?

4. What is an area of your division/
   department that is always underutilized
   or understaffed, or seems constantly
   overloaded?

5. What specific skills and resources
   would your organization's personnel
   need to fulfill your dreams? To meet
   its challenges?

6. Who in your circles of influence
   embraces volunteers and would be
   open to building the organization's
   capacity to address these dreams and
   challenges?

7. Who are your Mavens? Who are the experts on volunteering? On projects your organization wants to begin or complete?

8. Who are your Connectors? Who seems connected to everyone in particular communities you want to tap? (Which communities?)

9. Who are your Salespeople? Who can sell someone the shirt off her back and make her glad to buy it?

10. Are you an answer to any of the previous three questions? (Which ones? Why?)

11. With what could your organization utilize a consultant or specialist to help you—now and in the future—work toward vision and mission fulfillment?

12. What areas of your organization would benefit from program outcome evaluation?

Based on these Needs Assessment data, what are three entrepreneurial volunteer assignments or volunteer leadership positions that would be an asset to you and your organization?

1.

2.

3.

Work Plan

Vision Statement	Resources	Action	Yield	Initial Impact	Sustained Outcome

PROGRESS REPORT

Vision: _____

Element	Description	Indicators and Tools	Progress, Challenges, and Needs
Resources			
Action			
Yield			
Initial Impact			
Sustained Outcome			

Boomer Characteristic	Opportunities in My Organization
Demographics • Late retirement • Long life • Healthy late life • More women wage earners • Sandwich generation • Greater financial resources	

Behaviors
• Mobile in careers/relationships/
  locations/roles
• Long work hours
• Always "on call" for their jobs
• Gradual transition to retirement
• Less demanding encore careers
• Sabbatical after retirement and
  before volunteering	

Preferences/Motivations
• Passion for causes
• Desire to feel productive and
  see results
• Lifelong learners
• Want to leave a social legacy
• Want autonomy
• Want choices
• Want collaborative relationships
• Want to use their workplace skills
• Seek encore careers
• Minimal respect for authority
• Not joiners of social
  organizations; create their
  own connections	

Loosely adapted, with permission, from "Developing Compelling Opportunities for Baby Boomers," training handout, Temple University's Center for Intergenerational Learning, D. Scott Martin, author.[42]

Term Definitions

Episodic	Can be a onetime commitment or occasional participation.
Ongoing Episodic	Volunteers perceive that the assignment is low risk, low commitment, low responsibility, yet they return to the same assignment over and over.
Short-Term	Projects with a beginning, middle, and end, or a project that is very time specific over a short period of time.

Title, Description	Commitment	Considerations	Existing Positions We Could Retool and Ideas to Get It Done
Seasonal Work either in the season they are available or the season when they are needed	Episodic or short-term Organization's high-season assistance	• Availability • Skill requirements • Connection • Targeted recruitment efforts	
Substitute Provide coverage on an as-needed basis	On demand to fill in or be on-call	• Skill level • Availability • Scheduling • Self-direction	

Title, Description	Commitment	Considerations	Existing Positions We Could Retool and Ideas to Get It Done
Job Sharing Two or more volunteers share an assignment with either the same responsibilities or complementary responsibilities, depending on their skill set	Serve as one volunteer sharing responsibilities and splitting the time, providing coverage for each other; schedule can be prearranged or worked out among themselves	• Relationships • Communication • Teamwork • Self-direction • May need to recruit job share partners or have a volunteer recruit own job share partner	
Rotation Volunteers share the assignment by taking turns to accomplish tasks or responsibilities	Specified but negotiable	• Communication • Connection to the organization • Dependability	
Segmentation Divide a new or existing time and/or people-intensive task or position and break it into more manageable specific parts	Negotiated time commitment Can be time limited or ongoing	• Skill level • Relationships • Self-direction • Autonomy • Communication • Ability to work as a team	

Title, Description	Commitment	Considerations	**Existing Positions We Could Retool and Ideas to Get It Done**
Team Volunteering A group of self-directed volunteers taking on a project, program, or assignment	Time limited or ongoing Episodic or short-term	• Relationship • Community • Self-direction • Accountability	
Consultant Providing professional skills and content expertise to the organization	Usually time limited Schedule based on volunteer availability Could be episodic Could be virtual	• Skill level • Experience • Communication • Relationship • Self-directed • Autonomy • Strategic thinking	
Virtual Providing services to the organization from off-site location, utilizing technology such as phone, fax, Internet, or email	Schedule own time Time limited or ongoing	• Autonomy • Self-direction • Relationship • Communication • Skill level	

Position Overview

_____

_____

_____

Title: _____

Key responsibilities: _____

_____

_____

_____

Initial impact: _____

_____

_____

Sustained outcomes: _____

_____

_____

_____

Training: _____

_____

_____

_____

Support: _____

_____

_____

_____

_____

Commitment: _____

_____

_____

Length of time: _____

_____

Amount of time: _____

_____

Specify evenings, weekdays, weekends: _____

_____

Location of volunteer assignment: _____

_____

Qualifications: _____

_____

Skills: _____

_____

Benefits: _____

_____

_____

Case Statement for Boomer Volunteer Engagement

Element	Your Case Statement
Background on how initiative began and why it is a strategic priority	
Connection to organizational mission and vision	
Financial supporters, including stakeholders and powerful allies	
Examples: success stories and exemplary programs and services	

Element	Your Case Statement
Speaking Points	
	....
Elevator Speech	

Boomer Volunteer Engagement
Collaborate Today, Thrive Tomorrow

Title

_____

_____

Call-to-Action

_____

_____

_____

_____

_____

Position Overview

_____

_____

_____

_____

_____

_____

_____

_____

_____

_____

_____

_____

Motivational Analysis

Adapted with permission from *The Volunteer Development Toolbox: Tools and Techniques to Enhance Volunteer and Staff Effectiveness* by Gail Moore and Marilyn MacKenzie.

Each of the following sets of statements offers three choices. Check the one that most closely fits your own motivations. Remember, there are no wrong answers.

1. ___a. When doing a job, I seek feedback.
   ___b. I prefer to work alone and am eager to be my own boss.
   ___c. I feel less comfortable when forced to work alone.

2. ___a. I go out of my way to make friends with new people.
   ___b. I enjoy a good argument/debate.
   ___c. After starting a task, I am not comfortable until it is completed.

3. ___a. Status symbols are important to me.
   ___b. I am always getting involved in group projects.
   ___c. I work better when there is a deadline.

4. ___a. I work best when there is some challenge involved.
   ___b. I would rather give orders than take them.
   ___c. I am sensitive to others—especially when they are angry.

5. ___a. I am eager to be my own boss.
   ___b. I accept responsibility eagerly.
   ___c. I try to develop a personal relationship with my teammates.

6. ___a. I am uncomfortable when forced to work alone.
   ___b. I prefer being my own boss, even when others feel a joint effort is required.
   ___c. When given responsibility, I set measurable standards of high performance.

7. ___a. I am very concerned about my reputation or position.
   ___b. I have a desire to outperform others.
   ___c. I am concerned with being liked and accepted.

8. ___a. I enjoy and seek warm, friendly relationships.

   ___b. I attempt complete involvement on a project.

   ___c. I want my ideas to predominate.

9. ___a. I desire unique accomplishments.

   ___b. I like to work with others.

   ___c. I have a need and desire to influence others.

10. ___a. I think about consoling and helping others.

    ___b. I am verbally fluent.

    ___c. I am restless and innovative.

11. ___a. I set goals and think about how to attain them.

    ___b. I think about ways to challenge people.

    ___c. I think a lot about my feelings and the feelings of others.

Key: Check your answers. The style with the most answers is your primary style.

1. a. Achievement
   b. Power
   c. Affiliation

2. a. Affiliation
   b. Power
   c. Achievement

3. a. Power
   b. Affiliation
   c. Achievement

4. a. Achievement
   b. Power
   c. Affiliation

5. a. Power
   b. Achievement
   c. Affiliation

6. a. Affiliation
   b. Power
   c. Achievement

7. a. Power
   b. Achievement
   c. Affiliation

8. a. Affiliation
   b. Achievement
   c. Power

9. a. Achievement
   b. Affiliation
   c. Power

10. a. Affiliation
    b. Power
    c. Achievement

11. a. Achievement
    b. Power
    c. Affiliation

1. **Problem-Solving Question**

2. **Situational Question**

3. **Experiential Question**

4. **Skills Question**

Acknowledgment Tailored to Motivation

Motivation	Characteristics	Acknowledgment
Achievement	• Look for projects with a beginning, middle, and end • Want clear, concrete feedback • Are interested in assignments with the opportunity to solve problems • Seek assignments that are time limited • Want control over the outcome of the work	1. 2. 3. 4.
Power	• Seek assignments with significant and definable impact • Desire to have influence • Want to share their ideas • Are interested in prestige, status, and position	1. 2. 3. 4.
Affiliation	• Are interested in being with others • Friendship and relationships are a top priority • Desire a warm, friendly, and supportive work environment • Demonstrate concern and caring for others • Relationships may be more important than the work itself	1. 2. 3. 4.

Individual Volunteer Plan (IVP)

Volunteer's Name: _____ Date: _____

Support Liaison (Supervisor): _____

Current Competencies

1. _____

2. _____

3. _____

4. _____

5. _____

6. _____

Goals and Benchmarks

1. _____

2. _____

3. _____

4. _____

5. _____

6. _____

Additional Needs

1. _____

2. _____

3. _____

4. _____

5. _____

6. _____

Signatures

Volunteer:_____

Supporter (Supervisor): _____

Executive Director:_____

Board Chair: _____

Updates: _____

_____

_____

_____

Date for Next Progress Review: _____

_____

NOTES

Introduction

1   U.S. Census Bureau, Newsroom, *Special Feature: Oldest Boomer Turns 60*, 2006, http://www.census. gov/Press-Release/www/releases/archives/facts_for_features_special_editions/006105.html (accessed March 16, 2008).

2   Marlene Wilson, *The Effective Management of Volunteer Programs* (Boulder, CO: Volunteer Management Association, 1976), p. 7.

3   Dictionary.com, *Webster's New Millennium Dictionary of English*, Preview Edition (v 0.9.7). Lexico Publishing Group, LLC, 2003–2008, http://dictionary.reference.com/browse/Greatest Generation (accessed March 14, 2008).

4   Gail Sheehy, *New Passages* (New York: Random House, 1995), p. 29.

Chapter 1

5   Sources include Margaret Roberts et al., "Boomers Leading Change: Community Assessment," Rose Community Foundation, June 28, 2007, http://www.rcfdenver.org/initiatives_blc_info.htm (accessed March 14, 2008); Harvard School of Public Health–Metlife Foundation. "Reinventing Aging, Baby Boomer and Civic Engagement," Harvard School of Public Health–MetLife Foundation Initiative on Retirement & Civic Engagement, 2004, http://www.hsph.harvard.edu/ chc/reinventingaging/Report.pdf (accessed March 17, 2008); Peter D. Hart Research Associates, "Great Expectations: Boomers and the Future of Volunteering," Corporation for National & Community Service, 2007, http://www.civicengagement.org/agingsociety/links/07_0307_ boomer_report.pdf (accessed March 14, 2008);VolunteerMatch, 2007, http://www.volunteer-match.org/nonprofits/resources/greatexpectations (accessed March 14, 2008). The VolunteerMatch survey is limited to VolunteerMatch consumers.

6   Margaret Mark and Marvin Waldman, "Recasting Retirement: New Perspectives on Aging and Civic Engagement," Civic Ventures and Temple University Center for Intergenerational Learning, 2004, http://www.experiencecorps.org/images/pdf/Recast_Retire.pdf (accessed March 17, 2008).

7   Marc Freedman, *Encore: Finding Work That Matters in the Second Half of Life* (New York: Public Affairs, 2007).

8   Sara Davidson, *Leap! What Will We Do with the Rest of Our Lives? Reflections from the Boomer Generation* (New York: Random House, 2007).

9   Margaret Roberts et al., "Boomers Leading Change: Community Assessment," Rose Community Foundation, June 28, 2007, http://www.rcfdenver.org/initiatives_blc_info.htm (accessed March 14, 2008).

10   Peter D. Hart Research Associates, "Great Expectations: Boomers and the Future of Volunteering," VolunteerMatch, 2007, http://www.volunteermatch.org/nonprofits/resources/greatexpectations (accessed March 14, 2008).

11   John Foster-Bey et al., "Keeping Baby Boomers Volunteering," Corporation for National & Community Service, 2007, http://www.civicengagement.org/agingsociety/links/07_0307_ boomer_report.pdf (accessed March 14, 2008).

12 "Baby Boomer Facts," Corporation for National & Community Service, undated, http://www.getinvolved.gov/newsroom/press/factsheet_boomers.asp (accessed March 17, 2008).

13 Amy Ridenour, "The Debt Tsunami Begins: First Baby Boomer Files for Social Security," National Center for Public Policy Research, October 15, 2007, http://www.nationalcenter.org/2007/10/debt-tsunami-begins-first-baby-boomer.html (accessed March 16, 2008).

14 John Foster-Bey et al., "Keeping Baby Boomers Volunteering," Corporation for National & Community Service, 2007, http://www.civicengagement.org/agingsociety/links/07_0307_boomer_report.pdf (accessed March 14, 2008).

15 John J. Havens and Paul G. Schervish, "Why the $41 Trillion Wealth Transfer Estate Is Still Valid," Boston College Social Welfare Research Institute, January 6, 2003, http://www.bc.edu/bc_org/avp/gsas/swri/documents/$41trillionreview.pdf (accessed March 17, 2008).

16 Independent Sector, "Giving and Volunteering in the United States," 2001, http://www.independentsector.org/PDFs/GV01keyfind.pdf (accessed March 14, 2008).

17 Marc Freedman, *Encore: Finding Work That Matters in the Second Half of Life* (New York: Public Affairs, 2007), front flap.

18 Third Age, "Interview: Boomers May Lead a Longevity Revolution," http://www2.thirdage.com/articles/interview-boomers-may-lead-longevity-revolution (accessed March 15, 2008).

19 Jill Casner-Lotto, "Break Through Award Ceremony, Boomers Are Ready for Nonprofits, but Are Nonprofits Ready for Them?" The MetLife Foundation/Civic Ventures, 2007, http://www.civicventures.org/breakthrough/reports/ConfBdreport5-25.pdf (accessed March 15, 2008).

20 KVOA Tucson, "Senior Centers Retool for Boomer Retirees," December 2, 2005, http://www.kvoa.com/Global/story.asp?S=4193529 (accessed March 15, 2008).

21 Social networking sites include http://www.boomerChannels.com, http://www.boomertown.com, http://www.boomj.com, boomer-living.com/coffeehouse, http://www.eons.com, and http://www.rezoom.com, among others.

22 Marc Freedman, *Encore: Finding Work That Matters in the Second Half of Life* (New York: Public Affairs, 2007), p. 9.

23 Bureau of Labor Statistics, "Number of Jobs Held, Labor Market Activity, and Earnings Growth Among the Youngest Baby Boomers: Results from a Longitudinal Survey," United States Department of Labor, August 25, 2006, http://www.bls.gov/news.release/pdf/nlsoy.pdf (accessed March 15, 2008).

24 Nikki Harmon and Mairead Stack, "Boomers in the Workforce," Kleber & Associates, November 15, 2007, http://www.kleberandassociates.com/NewsBoomersinWorkplace.aspx (accessed March 15, 2008).

25 AARP Public Policy Institute, "Boomers Approaching Midlife: How Secure a Future?" AARP, 1998, http://assets.aarp.org/rgcenter/econ/d16687_boomers.pdf (accessed March 15, 2008).

26 Marc Freedman, *Encore: Finding Work That Matters in the Second Half of Life* (New York: Public Affairs, 2007), p. 150.

27 Ibid., pp. 185–186.

28 Dawn Lindblom, "Baby Boomers and the New Age of Volunteerism," Corporation for National & Community Service, July 17, 2001, http://www.nationalserviceresources.org/filemanager/download/465/lindblom.pdf (accessed March 15, 2008).

29 Peter D. Hart Research Associates, "Great Expectations: Boomers and the Future of Volunteering," VolunteerMatch, 2007, http://www.volunteermatch.org/nonprofits/resources/greatexpectations (accessed March 14, 2008); Margaret Roberts et al., "Boomers Leading Change: Community Assessment," Rose Community Foundation, June 28, 2007, http://www.rcfdenver.org/initiatives_blc_info.htm (accessed March 14, 2008); John Foster-Bey et al., "Keeping Baby Boomers Volunteering," Corporation for National & Community Service, 2007, www.civicengagement.org/agingsociety/links/07_0307_boomer_report.pdf (accessed March 14, 2008); Marc Freedman, *Encore: Finding Work That Matters in the Second Half of Life* (New York: Public Affairs, 2007), p. 119.

30 Marc Freedman, *Prime Time: How Baby Boomers Will Revolutionize Retirement and Transform America* (New York: Public Affairs, 1999), pp. 174–216.

31 Laura B. Wilson and Sharon P. Simpson, *Civic Engagement and the Baby Boomer Generation* (New York: The Haworth Press, 2006), pp. 85–109.

32 Robert D. Putnam, *Bowling Alone: The Collapse and Revival of American Community* (New York: Simon & Schuster, 2001), pp. 250–254.

33 Jill Casner-Lotto, "Break Through Award Ceremony, Boomers Are Ready for Nonprofits, but Are Nonprofits Ready for Them?" The MetLife Foundation/Civic Ventures, 2007, http://www.civicventures.org/breakthrough/reports/ConfBdreport5-25.pdf (accessed March 15, 2008).

34 Peter D. Hart Research Associates, "Great Expectations: Boomers and the Future of Volunteering," VolunteerMatch, 2007, http://www.volunteermatch.org/nonprofits/resources/greatexpectations (accessed March 14, 2008).

35 "Volunteer IMPACT Executive Study," Deloitte/Points of Light, 2006, http://www.deloitte.com/dtt/cda/doc/content/us_pointsoflight_executivesummary.pdf (accessed March 15, 2008).

36 Marc Freedman, *Encore: Finding Work That Matters in the Second Half of Life* (New York: Public Affairs, 2007), p. 155.

Chapter 2

37 William Bridges, *Managing Transitions: Making the Most of Change* (Cambridge, MA: Da Capo Press, 2003), pp. 23–75.

38 Malcolm Gladwell, *The Tipping Point: How Little Things Can Make a Big Difference* (New York: Back Bay Books/Little, Brown, 2002), pp. 30–88.

Chapter 3

39 Peter Senge, "The Fifth Discipline: The Art and Practice of the Learning Organization," Infed, undated, www.infed.org/thinkers/senge.htm (accessed March 15, 2008).

Chapter 4

40 Margaret Roberts et al., "Boomers Leading Change: Community Assessment," Rose Community Foundation, June 28, 2007, http://www.rcfdenver.org/initiatives_blc_info.htm (accessed March 14, 2008); Peter D. Hart Research Associates, "Great Expectations: Boomers and the Future of Volunteering," VolunteerMatch, 2007, http://www.volunteermatch.org/nonprofits/resources/greatexpectations (accessed March 14, 2008).

41 Ibid.

42 For more information, see D. Scott Martin, "Restructuring Current Volunteer Opportunities to Appeal to Baby Boomer Volunteers," Corporation for National & Community Service, undated, http://nationalserviceresources.org/epicenter/practices/snippet.php?action=print&ep_action=view&ep_id=1128 (accessed March 17, 2008).

Chapter 5

43 VolunteerMatch homepage, www.volunteermatch.org (accessed March 15, 2008).

44 "Social Networking Sites for Boomers Blossom," National Public Radio, September 17, 2007, www.npr.org/templates/story/story.php?storyId=14465186 (accessed March 17, 2008).

45 Ibid.

Chapter 6

46 John Foster-Bey et al., "Keeping Baby Boomers Volunteering," Corporation for National & Community Service, 2007, www.civicengagement.org/agingsociety/links/07_0307_boomer_report.pdf (accessed March 14, 2008).

47 Marlene Wilson, *The Effective Management of Volunteer Programs* (Boulder, CO: Volunteer Management Association, 1976), pp. 45–50.

48 Gail Moore and Marilyn MacKenzie, *The Volunteer Development Toolbox: Tools and Techniques to Enhance Volunteer and Staff Effectiveness* (Downers Grove, IL: Heritage Arts Publishing, 1993), pp. 20–30.

Chapter 8

49 Jill Friedman Fixler and Jennifer Rackow, "The Individual Volunteer Plan: Developing Top Volunteer Talent," Charity Channel, January 2, 2008, http://www.charitychannel.com (accessed March 16, 2008).

Chapter 9

50 John Foster-Bey et al., "Keeping Baby Boomers Volunteering," Corporation for National & Community Service, 2007, http://www.civicengagement.org/agingsociety/links/07_0307_boomer_report.pdf (accessed March 14, 2008).

51 "Volunteer IMPACT Executive Study," Deloitte/Points of Light, 2006, http://www.deloitte.com/dtt/cda/doc/content/us_pointsoflight_executivesummary.pdf (accessed March 15, 2008).

GLOSSARY

Acknowledgment: the expression of gratitude and appreciation for the personal contributions a volunteer or staff member has made through collaborative volunteer engagement, and the celebration of the results of his or her work.

Action: the portion of the volunteer engagement work plan that identifies the activities and tasks necessary to achieve goals.

Baby Boomer: a person born between 1946 and 1964, estimated to be 78.2 million individuals in the United States; also called Boomers.

Benchmarking: the process of establishing standards and milestones against which success and/or progress can be measured in the future; in volunteer engagement, the standards are best practices.

Best practices: the way of accomplishing a task that is both most efficient (requiring the least amount of effort) and effective (yielding the best results), based on repeatable procedures that have proven themselves over time for large numbers of people.

Boomer volunteer engagement competencies: key skills, characteristics, and assets that enable nonprofits to engage Baby Boomer volunteers successfully.

Boomer volunteer engagement task force: a group of key stakeholders who create the vision, shepherd the process, and are held accountable for the outcomes of the volunteer engagement work plan; preferably includes the CEO, selected board members, staff members, and high-impact volunteers.

Capacity building: mission-aligned, focused actions that improve the organization's effectiveness.

Case statement: a clear and concisely written communication of the vision for a cause, developed especially when launching a new organization or initiative, and refined as an organization ages and initiatives evolve.

Champions: an organization's existing innovators, risk takers, and most open-minded practitioners who are entrusted with the task of embracing and implementing a new policy or initiative and receive support to be successful.

Circle of influence: people who can impact a nonprofit, such as donors, board members, staff, clients, families, neighbors, stakeholders, partners, and volunteers. (See also **Stakeholders**.)

Cultivation: recognizing, fostering, and nurturing the growth or expansion of the resources that exist within an organization, including volunteers, donors, clients and their families, and event participants; also includes reaching out to potential volunteers through technology and traditional methods.

Elevator speech: an overview of an idea, initiative, product, or service designed to communicate a concept effectively in an engaging way in just a brief amount of time; a pitch.

Gatekeeper: the ambassador for a nonprofit who is the frontline contact for volunteers seeking information and/or placement within the organization.

Generation X: people born roughly during the years 1965 to 1980 in Western countries, especially the United States.

Greatest Generation: people born in the United States from about 1911 to 1924; the generation that fought in World War II and the Korean War.

Individual Volunteer Plan (IVP): mutually agreed-upon goals and benchmarks for a volunteer's work with a nonprofit, designed to map out a potential volunteer career path; an adaptation of an existing tool, the IEP, or Individual Education Plan.

Initial impact: significant, measurable change that occurs for the organization or its beneficiaries as outlined in a volunteer position description and a volunteer engagement work plan; examples include changes in knowledge, skills, competencies, attitudes, and behaviors.

Learning organization: coined by Peter Senge, an organization that systematically learns from its experience of what works and what does not work; the goal of learning is increased shared innovation, effectiveness, and performance.

Logic model: a framework for describing and understanding the work of a nonprofit, organized in four broad categories or steps, namely inputs, activities, outputs, and outcomes.

Millennial: person born between 1980 and 2000 (sources vary on the specific years for this generation; the definition is evolving).

Needs assessment: a process for determining the current status of an organization and for identifying its needs.

Negotiation: a conversation intended to produce a mutually acceptable agreement of terms and expectations.

Pilot program: small, carefully selected program charged with innovating and then testing those innovations; selected to transform organizations gradually, intentionally, and effectively by creating learning opportunities and leveraging internal champions.

Portal: The entry point through which volunteers first engage with a nonprofit, for example a website, event, phone call to the volunteer office, etc.

Position description: a detailed overview of a volunteer assignment, including a position overview, title, key responsibilities of the assignment, initial impact of the assignment, sustained outcome of the assignment, training, time commitment, service location options, desired qualifications, support, and benefits to the volunteer.

Progress report: a tool to measure the changes made by an initiative, as measured against the work plan; a means of communicating impacts to key stakeholders.

Recognition: a volunteer management method of showing appreciation for volunteer work through event-based, award-oriented actions that are directed from staff to volunteers.

Resources: the portion of the volunteer engagement work plan that identifies what is needed before the action can occur, including people, training, supplies, equipment, money, time, and space.

Risk management: a structured approach to mitigating risk.

Sandwich Generation: a generation of people who care for their aging parents while supporting their own children.

Silent Generation: people born in the United States between 1925 and 1944, between the two world wars.

Skills: proficiencies and talents that may have been developed through unrelated experiences and are transferable.

Social legacy: a humanitarian contribution left as a monument to past generations and as a gift to future generations.

Social networking website: an online platform that convenes communities of people with shared interests and activities or who are interested in connecting with others; much of the content is user generated.

Stakeholders: individuals with a personal investment in the nonprofit, such as donors, board members, staff, clients, families, neighbors, partners, and volunteers.

Support: encouragement and nurturing of volunteers to ensure that the volunteers' needs and the nonprofit's goals are met.

Sustainability: the ability to maintain an ongoing state.

Task force: a group of people and resources temporarily brought together for a specific purpose.

Virtual volunteering: Volunteers providing services to a nonprofit from an off-site location, utilizing technology such as phone, fax, Internet, or email.

Vision: a vivid description of what a nonprofit can become if it fulfills its strategic initiatives and operations into the future.

Volunteer engagement: a people-centered model for achieving mission fulfillment that aligns volunteers' needs and proficiencies with the nonprofit's vision, mission, and goals; volunteer engagement is collaborative; leaders of volunteers focus on volunteers' personal motivations and passions and then invite volunteers to strengthen the nonprofit by doing what they love and what their skills enable.

Volunteer management: a position-centered model of utilizing volunteers in predetermined positions, designed by staff and driven by staff needs.

Volunteer matching search engine: websites designed to provide listings of available volunteer positions and to match potential volunteers with organizations.

Work plan: a roadmap for implementation of an initiative, program, or other organizational effort, identifying action steps and indicators for performance measurement.

Yield: quantifiable results of actions.

RESOURCES

AARP Public Policy Institute. "Boomers Approaching Midlife: How Secure a Future?" AARP, 1998. http://assets.aarp.org/rgcenter/econ/d16687_boomers.pdf (accessed March 15, 2008).

Adler, Jerry. "The Boomer Files." *Newsweek*, November 14, 2005. Also available online at http://agewave.com/media_files/newsweek111405.html (accessed March 16, 2008).

Axelrod, Richard H. *Terms of Engagement: Changing the Way We Change Organizations.* San Francisco: Berrett-Koehler Publishers, 2000.

The Bamboo Project. "Using Facebook in Your Nonprofit." The Bamboo Project, undated. http://michelemartin.typepad.com/thebambooprojectblog/2007/04/some_resources_.html (accessed March 17, 2008).

Bressler, Jeanette, Kristi Jackson, Evelyn Montalvo, and Nancy Z. Henkin. "Coming of Age: Focus Group Summary Report: Understanding How Philadelphians Age 50+ View Volunteerism." Temple University Center for Intergenerational Learning, 2004. http://www.comingofage. org/documents/coa_color_focus_group_report.pdf (accessed March 17, 2008).

Bridges, William. *Managing Transitions: Making the Most of Change.* Cambridge, MA: Da Capo Press, 2003.

Bronfman Edgar. *The Third Act: Reinventing Yourself After Retirement.* New York: G. P. Putnam's Sons, 2002.

Bureau of Labor Statistics. "Number of Jobs Held, Labor Market Activity, and Earnings Growth Among the Youngest Baby Boomers: Results from a Longitudinal Survey." United States Department of Labor, August 25, 2006. http://www.bls.gov/news.release/pdf/nlsoy.pdf (accessed March 15, 2008).

Casner-Lotto, Jill. "Break Through Award Ceremony, Boomers Are Ready for Nonprofits, but Are Nonprofits Ready for Them?" The MetLife Foundation/Civic Ventures, 2007. http://www. civicventures.org/breakthrough/reports/ConfBdreport5-25.pdf (accessed March 15, 2008).

Civic Ventures. http://www.civicventures.org (accessed March 16, 2008).

———. "Blueprint for the Next Chapter." Civic Ventures, May 2005. http://www.civicventures. org/publications/booklets/Blueprint.pdf (accessed March 26, 2008).

————."Civic Trends: Boomers by the Numbers." Civic Ventures, undated. http://www.
civicventures.org/publications/articles/boomers_by_the_numbers.cfm (accessed March 16,
2008).

————. "Civic Ventures Overview: Leading with Experience." Civic Ventures, undated.
http://www.civicventures.org/overview.cfm (accessed March 14, 2008).

————. "Realizing the Experience Dividend: Helping the Longevity Revolution Add Up for
America." Civic Ventures, 2006 (accessed March 17, 2008).

————. "Ten Ways Your Organization Can Realize an Experience Dividend." Civic Ventures,
undated. http://www.civicventures.org/publications/articles/TenWays (accessed March 17,
2008).

Coming of Age Incorporated. "Marketing to Baby Boomers." Coming of Age Incorporated, undated.
http://www.comingofage.com/marketing-baby-boomers.htm (accessed March 26, 2008).

Corporation for National & Community Service. "Baby Boomer Facts." Corporation for National &
Community Service, undated. http://www.getinvolved.gov/newsroom/press/factsheet_
boomers.asp (accessed March 17, 2008).

————. "Finding Innovative Volunteer Opportunities for Baby Boomers." Corporation for
National & Community Service, 2004. http://nationalserviceresources.org/epicenter/
practices/snippet.php?action=print&ep_action=view&ep_id=984 (accessed March 17, 2008).

————. "Volunteering Reinvented: Human Capital Solutions for the Nonprofit Sector."
Corporation for National & Community Service, July 2007. http://www.iave.org/
resources/07_0719_volunteering_reinvented.pdf (accessed March 17, 2008).

Davidson, Sara. *Leap! What Will We Do with the Rest of Our Lives? Reflections from the Boomer
Generation.* New York: Random House, 2007.

Deloitte/Points of Light. "Volunteer IMPACT Executive Study." Deloitte/Points of Light, 2006.
http://www.deloitte.com/dtt/cda/doc/content/us_pointsoflight_executivesummary.pdf
(accessed March 15, 2008).

Denison, Dwight, and Ashley Moore. "Using Baby Boomers to Expand Nonprofit Capacity."
Journal for Nonprofit Management, 2007. http://www.supportcenteronline.org/images/
babyboomers.pdf (accessed March 17, 2008).

Dictionary.com. *Webster's New Millennium Dictionary of English,* Preview Edition (v 0.9.7). Lexico
Publishing Group, LLC. http://dictionary.reference.com/browse/Greatest Generation
(accessed March 14, 2008).

DIOSA/Communications. "MySpace Best Practices." DIOSA/Communications, undated. http://www.diosacommunications.com/myspacebestpractices.htm (accessed March 17, 2008).

Drucker, Paul F. *Management Challenges for the 21st Century.* New York: HarperCollins, 1999.

Dychtwald, Ken. *Age Wave: How the Most Important Trend of Our Time Will Change Your Future.* New York: Bantam Books, 1990.

El-Borno, Soha. "A Beginner's Guide to Facebook: How Nonprofits Can Get Started on the Popular Social Networking Site." Techsoup, August 16, 2007. http://www.techsoup.org/ learning center/internet/page7430.cfm?cg=searchterms&sg=facebook (accessed March 16, 2008).

———. "Promote Your Cause on Facebook in Six Easy Steps: How to Reach Out Using Facebook's New Causes Application." Techsoup, August 15, 2007. http://www.techsoup.org/learning center/internet/page7416.cfm?cg=searchterms&sg=facebook (accessed March 17, 2008).

Fixler, Jill Friedman. "Capacity Building Part 1: Building Nonprofit Organizational Capacity Through Civic Engagement." Charity Channel, March 14, 2007. http://www.charitychannel. com (accessed March 16, 2008).

———. "Capacity Building Part 2: Creating a Tipping Point for Change." Charity Channel, March 18, 2007. http://www.charitychannel.com (accessed March 16, 2008).

Fixler, Jill Friedman, and Jennifer Rackow. "The Individual Volunteer Plan: Developing Top Volunteer Talent." Charity Channel, January 2, 2008. http://charitychannel.com (accessed March 16, 2008).

Foster-Bey, John, Robert Grimm, and Nathan Dietz. "Keeping Baby Boomers Volunteering." Corporation for National & Community Service, 2007. http://www.civicengagement.org/ agingsociety/links/07_0307_boomer_report.pdf (accessed March 14, 2008).

Freedman, Marc. "America's Untapped Resource." Civic Ventures, undated. http://www.civic ventures.org/publications/articles/americas_untapped_resource.cfm (accessed March 16, 2008).

———. *Encore/Finding Work That Matters in the Second Half of Life.* New York: Public Affairs, 2007.

———. *Prime Time: How Baby Boomers Will Revolutionize Retirement and Transform America.* New York: Public Affairs, 1999.

———. "Take Advantage of Us." Civic Ventures, 2004. http://www.civicventures.org/publications/ articles/take_advantage_of_us.cfm (accessed March 17, 2008).

Freudenheim, Ellen. "The Boomers' Guide to Good Work." The MetLife Foundation/Civic Ventures, 2008. www.civicventures.org/publications/booklets/boomers_guide.cfm (accessed March 16, 2008).

Gerencher, Kristen. "Boomer Volunteers Demanding Higher-Level Work: Nonprofits Advised to Accommodate Influential Group's Preferences." Market Watch, March 7, 2007. http://www.marketwatch.com/news/story/baby-boomers-demanding-higher-level-volunteer/story.aspx?guid=%7BB94A5269-C84A-4483-AA06-D96C727F4B12%7D (accessed March 17, 2008).

Gladwell, Malcolm. *The Tipping Point: How Little Things Can Make a Big Difference.* New York: Back Bay Books/Little, Brown, 2002.

Hands On Network. http://www.handsonnetwork.org (accessed March 17, 2008).

Harmon, Nikki, and Mairead Stack. "Boomers in the Workforce." Kleber & Associates, November 15, 2007. http://www.kleberandassociates.com/NewsBoomersinWorkplace.aspx (accessed March 15, 2008).

Harvard School of Public Health–Metlife Foundation. "Reinventing Aging, Baby Boomer and Civic Engagement." Harvard School of Public Health–MetLife Foundation Initiative on Retirement & Civic Engagement, 2004. http://www.hsph.harvard.edu/chc/reinventingaging/Report.pdf (accessed March 17, 2008).

Havens, John J., and Paul G. Schervish. "Why the $41 Trillion Wealth Transfer Estate Is Still Valid." Boston College Social Welfare Research Institute, January 6, 2003. http://www.bc.edu/bc_org/avp/gsas/swri/documents/$41trillionreview.pdf (accessed March 17, 2008).

Hoodless, Elisabeth. "Senior Volunteers: Solutions Waiting to Happen." Service Enquiry, undated. http://www.service-enquiry.org.za/downloads/chapter%206.pdf (accessed March 17, 2008).

Immersion Interactive. "White Pagers and Newsletters." Immersion Interactive, The Digital Boomer Agency. http://www.immersionactive.com/lower.cfm?section=resources&page=whitepapers (accessed March 16, 2008).

Independent Sector. "Giving and Volunteering in the United States." Independent Sector, 2001. http://www.independentsector.org/PDFs/GV01keyfind.pdf (accessed March 14, 2008).

Independent Sector and AARP. "Experience at Work: Volunteering and Giving among Americans 50 and Over." Independent Sector and AARP, 2008. http://www.independentsector.org/programs/research/experience.html (accessed March 17, 2008).

Johnson, Christopher, Mei Cobb, Miriam Parel, Marie Bouvier, and Jennifer Fauss. "50+ Volunteering: Working for Stronger Communities." Points of Light Foundation, 2004. http://www.pointsoflight.org/downloads/pdf/networks/olderadultWorkingForStronger Communities.pdf (accessed March 16, 2008).

Kelly, Colleen. *The Road Not Taken—Using Entrepreneurial Volunteers*. Philadelphia: Energize, Inc., 2004.

KVOA Tucson. "Senior Centers Retool for Boomer Retirees." December 2, 2005. http://www. kvoa.com/Global/story.asp?S=4193529 (accessed March 15, 2008).

Lindblom, Dawn. "Baby Boomers and the New Age of Volunteerism." Corporation for National & Community Service, July 17, 2001. http://nationalserviceresources.org/filemanager/download/ 465/lindblom.pdf (accessed March 15, 2008).

Lions International. "Recruiting the Baby Boom Generation: A Resource Guide." Lions International, undated. http://www.lionsclubs.org/boomers/pdfs/recruiting_guide.pdf (accessed March 17, 2008).

Mark, Margaret, and Marvin Waldman."Recasting Retirement: New Perspectives on Aging and Civic Engagement." Civic Ventures and Temple University Center for Intergenerational Learning, 2004. www.experiencecorps.org/images/pdf/Recast_Retire.pdf (accessed March 17, 2008).

Martin, D. Scott. "Baby Boomers, Adult Service Learning and Transformative Volunteer Experiences, Part 1." Charity Channel, July 12, 2006. http://www.charitychannel.com (accessed March 16, 2008).

———. "Creating Boomer-Friendly Volunteer Opportunities, Part 1: Restructuring Existing Opportunities." Charity Channel, January 18, 2006. http://www.charitychannel.com (accessed March 17, 2008).

———. "Creating Boomer-Friendly Volunteer Opportunities, Part 2: Developing Skilled Short-Term Projects." Charity Channel, February 8, 2006. http://www.charitychannel.com (accessed March 17, 2008).

———. "Creating Boomer-Friendly Volunteer Opportunities, Part 3: Groups." Charity Channel, February 15, 2006. http://www.charitychannel.com (accessed March 17, 2008).

———. "From 'Us and Them' to 'We': Participative Organizational Culture." Charity Channel, March 28, 2007. http://www.charitychannel.com (accessed March 17, 2008).

————. "Participative Visions in Volunteer Management: Selected Quotations (Part 2)." Charity Channel, December 6, 2006. http://www.charitychannel.com (accessed March 17, 2008).

————. "Participative Volunteer Management: The Emerging Paradigm? (Part 1)." Charity Channel, November 8, 2006. http://www.charitychannel.com (accessed March 17, 2008).

————. "Restructuring Current Volunteer Opportunities to Appeal to Baby Boomer Volunteers." Corporation for National & Community Service, undated. http://nationalserviceresources. org/epicenter/practices/snippet.php?action=print&ep_action=view&ep_id=1128 (accessed March 17, 2008).

————. "Talking to Baby Boomers About Volunteering, Part 1: Third Quarter of Life Passions." Charity Channel, November 2, 2005. http://www.charitychannel.com (accessed March 16, 2007).

————. "Talking to Baby Boomers About Volunteering, Part 2: Volunteering as a Career Transition Strategy." Charity Channel, November 16, 2005. http://www.charitychannel.com (accessed March 16, 2008).

Merrill Associates. http://www.merrillassociates.net (accessed March 17, 2008).

Meyer, Brett. "How To: Put Technology to Use (February 2008)." NTEN, Nonprofit Technology, undated. http://nten.org/blog/2008/02/25/how-to-put-technology-to-use-february-2008 (accessed March 26, 2008).

Meyer, Marc. "The Top 30 Social Network Sites for Baby Boomers." Emerson Direct Marketing Observations, November 13, 2007. http://emersondirect.wordpress.com/2007/11/13/the-top-30-social-network-sites-for-baby-boomers (accessed March 26, 2008).

National Public Radio. "Social Networking Sites for Boomers Blossom." NPR, September 17, 2007. http://www.npr.org/templates/story/story.php?storyId=14465186 (accessed March 17, 2008).

Peter D. Hart Research Associates. "Great Expectations: Boomers and the Future of Volunteering." VolunteerMatch, 2007. http://www.volunteermatch.org/nonprofits/resources/great expectations (accessed March 14, 2008).

Points of Light Foundation. http://www.pointsoflight.org (accessed March 17, 2008).

Prisuta, Robert. "Enhancing Volunteerism Among Aging Boomers." AARP, October 2003. http:// assets.aarp.org/rgcenter/general/boomers_engagement_2.pdf (accessed March 26, 2008).

Putnam, Robert D. *Bowling Alone: The Collapse and Revival of American Community.* New York: Simon & Schuster, 2001.

Ridenour, Amy. "The Debt Tsunami Begins: First Baby Boomer Files for Social Security." National Center for Public Policy Research, October 15, 2007. http://www.nationalcenter.org/2007/10/debt-tsunami-begins-first-baby-boomer.html (accessed March 16, 2008).

Roberts, Margaret, Janine Vanderburg, Robin Leake, and Rose Prieto. "Boomers Leading Change: Community Assessment." Rose Community Foundation, June 28, 2007. http://www.rcfdenver.org/initiatives_blc_info.htm (accessed March 14, 2008).

Senge, Peter. *The Fifth Discipline: The Art and Practice of the Learning Organization.* New York: Currency/Doubleday, 1990.

———. "The Fifth Discipline: The Art and Practice of the Learning Organization." Infed, undated. http://www.infed.org/thinkers/senge.htm (accessed March 15, 2008).

Sheehy, Gail. *New Passages.* New York: Random House, 1995.

"Silver Surfers Are Catching the Social Networking Wave." *Mature Interaction,* Newsletter, April 12, 2007. http://www.videnbank.info/fulltext/4081.pdf (accessed March 17, 2008).

Spiegelman, Rande. "Baby Boomer Reality Check." Charles Schwab, April 18, 2007. http://www.schwab.com/public/schwab/research_strategies/market_insight/retirement_strategies/planning/baby_boomer_reality_check.html?cmsid=P-1006969&lvl1=research strategies&lvl2= market_insight&refid=P-1052799&refpid=P-1004666 (accessed March 13, 2008).

Stolworth, Della, Bandana Shrestha, and Miriam Parel. "Paving the Way: Volunteer Centers and Baby Boomer Volunteering." Points of Light Foundation, April 27, 2006. http://www.pointsoflight.org/downloads/pdf/programs/50plus/PavingtheWay_web1.pdf (accessed March 17, 2008).

Third Age. "Interview: Boomers May Lead a Longevity Revolution." http://www2.thirdage.com/articles/interview-boomers-may-lead-longevity-revolution (accessed March 15, 2008).

U.S. Census Bureau Newsroom. "Special Feature: Oldest Boomer Turns 60." U.S. Census Bureau, 2006. http://www.census.gov/Press-Release/www/releases/archives/facts_for_features_special_editions/006105.html (accessed March 16, 2008).

VolunteerMatch. http://www.volunteermatch.org (accessed March 15, 2008).

Wilson, Laura B., and Sharon P. Simson. *Civic Engagement and the Baby Boomer Generation.* New York: The Haworth Press, 2006.

Wilson, Marlene. *The Effective Management of Volunteer Programs.* Boulder, CO: Volunteer Management Association, 1976.

Selected Social Networking Sites Targeted to Boomers

Boomer Channels. http://www.boomerChannels.com (accessed March 26, 2008).

Boomer-Living. http://boomer-living.com/coffeehouse/(accessed March 26, 2008).

Boomers International. http://www.boomersint.org/ (accessed March 26, 2008).

Boomertown. http://www.boomertown.com/(accessed March 26, 2008).

BoomJ. http://www.boomj.com/ (accessed March 26, 2008).

Eons. http://www.eons.com/ (accessed March 26, 2008).

Selected Social Networking Sites

Facebook. http://www.facebook.com/(accessed March 26, 2008).

LinkedIn. http://www.linkedin.com/ (accessed March 26, 2008).

MySpace. http://www.myspace.com/ (accessed March 26, 2008).

ABOUT THE AUTHORS

Jill Friedman Fixler is a nationally known leader recognized for her innovative approaches to strengthening nonprofit organizations. She combines her skills as a consultant, trainer, facilitator, public speaker, and coach to promote excellence in volunteer engagement, strategic planning, and board and organizational development for nonprofit organizations across the United States. Jill has more than thirty years of experience, and the nonprofits she has worked with include health, human services, religious, government, cultural, environmental, and animal welfare organizations, and community centers. Jill has presented at numerous national and regional conferences, including the National Multiple Sclerosis Society Leadership Conference, the Hostelling International–USA National Council Meeting, the International Conference on Volunteer Administration, the American Cancer Society Western Regional Conference, and the Volunteers of America Colorado Leadership Conference. Based in Denver, she was a founding board member of both the Colorado AIDS Project and Metro Volunteers. Jill's many articles on volunteer management and board development have appeared in *Volunteer Management Review*, *E-Volunteerism Journal*, and *Nonprofit Boards and Governance Review*. For more information about JFFixler & Associates, go to www.jffixler.com.

Sandie Eichberg has more than twenty years of experience in volunteer engagement. She has taught online courses in volunteer engagement and served as a volunteer coordinator. Her work in a social service agency resulted in substantive growth of the volunteer corps. As an associate of JFFixler & Associates, Sandie specializes in faith-based volunteer engagement.

Gail Lorenz, CVA, has worked since 1989 in the nonprofit organization arena. Since 1998, she has been the Administrator of Volunteer Services for Colorado Legal Services in Denver, Colorado. She has provided training at the Colorado State Mental Health Conference, the Mental Health Association Conference, Denver Directors of Volunteers in Agencies, and Metro Volunteers. She has been a board member of Denver DOVIA and has worked on the regional and international conference planning committees for the Association of Volunteer Administration.

LaVergne, TN USA
09 October 2009
160364LV00001B/27/P

9 781434 385901